# WHAT HAVE YOU DONE FOR ME LATELY?

## THE INS AND OUTS OF NEW YORK POLITICS

# WHAT HAVE YOU DONE FOR ME LATELY?

## THE INS AND OUTS
## OF NEW YORK CITY POLITICS

by
Warren Moscow

PRENTICE-HALL, INC., Englewood Cliffs, N. J.

*What Have You Done For Me Lately? The Ins and Outs of New York City Politics* by Warren Moscow

© 1967 by Prentice-Hall, Inc.

Library of Congress Catalog Card Number: 67-15177

Printed in the United States of America

T 95215

Prentice-Hall International, Inc., *London*
Prentice-Hall of Australia, Pty. Ltd., *Sydney*
Prentice-Hall of Canada, Ltd., *Toronto*
Prentice-Hall of India Private Ltd., *New Delhi*
Prentice-Hall of Japan, Inc., *Tokyo*

*For John*

# CONTENTS

vii

# INTRODUCTION

This is the story of New York politics as I know it—the result of almost forty years exposure to it. Very little of the story will be found in the newspaper clippings, even my own. People inevitably will ask why I did not write it all as news at the time it happened. The answer lies in any one of three reasons: either I did not know what was going on; or the pattern of events was not clear enough for informed interpretation; or the part that I did know and did not report was obtained in confidence, from which I now feel released by the tolling of the years.

The men in government and politics who are or ought to be news sources hesitate to bare their real thinking or record their in-the-room conversations for publication while an issue is current. They like the privilege of privacy for themselves and hate to violate it even for an opponent. The linen, clean or dirty, should not be washed in public. When they trust a reporter, they will tell him much in confidence, imposing limits on the parts he may use.

The reporter learns to be wary of too much in confidence. It can cramp his style, preventing him from using the story even after it comes to him from another direction. Yet in the course of relations with his news sources, he cannot avoid be-

Introduction

ing party to confidences. Some politicians have trusted a selected reporter here and there to the point of giving him access
to the entire situation, and letting the reporter judge how
much he can use without hurting the news source. It has happened to me. Satisfactory as this is to the ego, and insuring as
it does the reporter's ability to draw an accurate picture of
things to come, it tends to make him lean backwards on details and motivation. He also must be leery of the politician
who gives him propaganda disguised as "off the record" information.

But in the normal course of events the reporter who works
at his job keeps reasonably well informed and can report
enough of what is happening to satisfy both his editors and
his readers. If he is both lucky and assiduous, he will be able
to piece in more and more bits of the mosaic in the weeks,
months and years that follow, as background for other news
to come.

When I started work on this book I refreshed my recollec-
tion of dates and situations by re-reading the clippings of my
own signed reports in *The New York Times* for the years
1930 through 1952, graciously turned over to me by *The
Times'* editors. I was impressed with how close I had gotten to
the truth, but was struck even more with what I had not
known as I wrote for the next morning deadline.

It makes all the more amazing the instant interpretation not
only demanded of, but furnished by, the reporters for today's
newspapers and radio and television networks. For on the day
a story breaks, sometimes even the news sources, the men involved, don't really know the whole story. Sometimes the beginning and the end of a story come from different sources,
based on different episodes many years apart.

The story of Mayor Jimmy Walker's jaunty defiance of his

# Introduction

Cardinal occurred in 1926. It was related at the time, in confidence, by the late Charles F. Kerrigan, Walker's assistant, to one reporter, James A. Hagerty of *The Times*. Hagerty passed the confidence to me, anecdotally, after I joined *The Times* staff in 1930. It was the first I knew of it, although I had been a fledgling City Hall reporter when it occurred. In 1932 I wrote the story, the day it happened, of the turning down of Walker for re-nomination by Tammany at the behest of the Catholic hierarchy. The Tammany leadership had given me, sub rosa, but for purposes of publication, the necessary interpretation of a Church statement just issued. When I thus wrote the 1932 finis to Walker's career, I still was bound by the inherited confidence of 1926.

The readers in 1932 were supplied with the necessary information, along with an outline of the reasoning, with a six year lapse between the opening and closing chapters, and the intimate details omitted.

The astounding story of the $200,000 bribe offered to Ed Flynn by a bootlegger had no circulation at all, even among politicians. It was dropped casually to me by Flynn, twenty-five years after the fact, in the course of our discussing something else. While newspapermen had recognized that gang wars had been kept out of The Bronx, and had attributed it to the Flynn-selected Bronx District Attorney, none of us ever knew Flynn's personal part, who he told off and how.

The story of the underworld in politics was one that was pieced together slowly, and the key pieces in the jigsaw did not fall into place for me until after I had ceased political reporting and was in politics myself.

In general, the bulk of the situations and the stories which illustrate them came to me during the twenty-six years I spent in the business of political reporting and the eleven years thereafter, in and out of city government. In many cases I have felt released from bonds of confidence by the deaths of the participants. In dealing from the inside with city affairs, I have not divulged anything that came to me in confidence because of the positions I held, but I have included matter which I observed without being a participant or which came to me without restriction.

For the perspective and anecdotes of earlier years of this century, I have relied on information passed on to me by two of the great reporters of the era. One was the above-mentioned James A. Hagerty, often now confused with his able son who was Eisenhower's press secretary. Old Jim started covering politics in New York for Bennett's *Herald* in 1910, and was still covering it fifty years later for *The Times*. He was properly the most respected and trusted political reporter of all time. The second was Charles S. Hand, also deceased. He was the brilliant political writer for the old *World*, served as Walker's press secretary, worked later for years on political campaigns and finally was my own immediate predecessor as Commissioner of Borough Works of Manhattan. His perspective was always of the finest. I cherished the friendship and trust of both as I valued the education they gave me.

In the actual preparation of this book, I owe a debt, as always, to my wife Jean for her constant affectionate encouragement; to my editorial assistant on *The New York Law Journal*, Jeffrey R. Bernstein, for his friendly and valuable criticism in his self-assigned role as guinea pig; and lastly to Robert Simpson, one of the finest copy editors who ever graced a newspaper desk, who gave the originally rougher chapters his skilled and tender care.

W.M.

May 1966

# 1. All the King's Horses

New York has been the nation's metropolis for approximately a century and a half. Whatever any other city has, New York has more of; be it gay or sad, good or criminal, plain or fancy. It is the city of O. Henry, E. B. White and Jimmy Breslin, the Mecca of youth seeking glamour, fame and fortune. It is the place people come to visit with the words formed in their minds in advance that they would never live in it.

But people do live there, work there and vote there. Many have even been born there and never left. Whether native, as Al Smith or Jimmy Walker, immigrant as O'Dwyer, or an adult returnee as Fiorello H. La Guardia, they contributed over the decades to a political and governmental scene as vivid, active and confusing as Times Square itself on a rainy night, with its screeching taxicabs, shining theater marquees, and pedestrians crossing against the lights.

In the world of politics, it is the biggest bloc of urban votes that often determines the electoral vote of the entire state. Yet legend has it that it wasn't reaction to the cry of

"Rum, Romanism and Rebellion" which cost New York State and the presidency to James G. Blaine; it was the votes that John Y. McKane stole for the Democratic ticket and Cleveland in the rum-soaked, sin-ridden village of Coney Island, one of several communities which had the Tammany spirit even before becoming part of the greater city.

To understand New York politics today one has to go back to how it started.

The City is the sum of a confederation of smaller cities, towns, villages and farmlands which had their own governments and interests as diverse as America's original thirteen colonies, or maybe the Holy Roman Empire.

To the rest of the world it may be Megalopolis, Gotham or Gomorrah. To those who intimately and actively take part in its government and politics, and also the run-of-the-mill voter, it consists of neighborhoods and villages—Flatbush and Flushing, Marble Hill and Astoria, Greenwich Village and Tottenville—housed for governmental purposes in five groups called boroughs that are themselves coterminous with five separate counties.

The spirit of confederation rather than merger was written into its civic life in 1898 when the conglomeration first came into being as "Greater New York," the largest city in the world. The retention of it has complicated its politics and served to divide its politicians right up to the present. Even its gangs and racketeers observe the borough boundaries.

The Democratic party is, and always has been, the dominant political party in New York, but there is no New York City Democratic party as such. Instead it has five groups, sometimes united, often divided, and central leadership occurs only by accident. The same is true for the Republicans. Only the old Socialist, American Labor and Communist parties, and the existing Liberals and Conservatives—all of which claimed to peddle philosophy rather than patronage or power—ever have worked consistently under centralized direction.

The proof is there at any period of the city's history. It was hardly in existence a dozen years when the boss of the Kings County Democracy (Brooklyn) snarled publicly at the leader of Manhattan's Tammany Hall that "the Tiger shall not cross the bridge."

In the 1940's, William O'Dwyer, as a Mayor who stemmed from Brooklyn, could use his power to change the leadership of his party in his home bailiwick. But when Robert F. Wagner, also Mayor, but strictly from Manhattan, tried the same thing in the same Brooklyn in the early 1960's, he was licked before he started. To the Brooklyn Democrats he was just an outsider butting in where he didn't belong.

Similarly, Edward J. Flynn, Boss of The Bronx, could support Franklin Delano Roosevelt for the presidential nomination in 1932 even though Tammany Boss John F. Curry and Brooklyn Boss John H. McCooey were fighting Roosevelt with fury and venom. Even if they had won, and Flynn had turned out to be backing a loser, their influence could never have crossed the Harlem and hurt him locally.

Because this built-in local independence is the key to so many of the city's political and governmental idiosyncrasies, it is worthwhile looking at the five boroughs: Manhattan, Brooklyn, The Bronx, Queens and Richmond, each with a Borough President representing it in the city government. Mayor James J. Walker used to refer to the borough presidents as "the five little mayors." Though their wings have been clipped again and again, the spirit of locality from which the concept sprang has never vanished.

3

## All the King's Horses

The original city, dignified as such by title when its population was only 800 and its name was Nieuw Amsterdam, lay at the southern tip of Manhattan Island, a sliver of land running roughly north-south for a maximum distance of 13.4 miles, and east-west for a maximum width of 2.3 miles. Peter Minuit supposedly traded $24 of beads and trinkets for the whole thing.

Today, it is the highest-priced real estate in the world, with its most sought land selling as high as $10,000,000 an acre. The increase in value stems from its original asset, its location as the perfect port and trading post, dedicated then, as now, to commerce. It has the great hospitable harbor at its foot; the broad avenue of the Hudson on the west; the tidal estuary of the East River furnishing a water route to New England via Long Island Sound. To the north the narrow, canalized Harlem River puts the final limit on its acres and separates it from the North American mainland.

More than a century ago, when America became the goal of Europe's poor and persecuted, New York was the natural port of entry for those millions of immigrants, and many lighted where they landed, in Manhattan. As the population mushroomed, particularly in the 1880's and 1890's, the original city pushed northward. But it didn't progress block by block along the streets which had been mapped and left as guides, as early as 1810. Instead, it leapfrogged rather than swallowed the early villages like Greenwich, Manhattanville, Haarlem, Bloomingdale and Yorkville, so that they retained their established identities.

The first acquisition of new territory came in 1874 with the purchase—at the cost of taking over bonded debt hastily created by the local yokels—of parts of Westchester County containing the hamlets of Morrisania, West Farms and Kingsbridge, territory loosely referred to as The Bronx. The rest of The Bronx was similarly annexed in 1895, while the peoples of Long Island and Staten Island, as well as Manhattan, were debating the merits of the bigger confederation, as they had been for a decade already. The matter was settled affirmatively by a referendum in 1897.

So, as of January 1, 1898, the major state, in terms of both wealth and population, in the new confederation consisted of the then existing City of New York, contained in the County of New York. For the purposes of the new set-up, however, it was divided into two boroughs, Manhattan and The Bronx, with the Harlem River as the dividing line. Manhattan's 22.6 square miles contained most of the 1,957,000 population. This reached slum density where the Eastern European immigrants herded on the lower East Side, but it was also scattered about the island in the old villages and on farms and fashionable estates. The 43.1 square miles of The Bronx, outside the hamlets, was mostly hills and rocks.

The Bronx, having been given status as a separate borough in 1898, when the borough idea was brand-new, won status as a county of the same name in 1913. Its secession from Manhattan was with Tammany's full consent. As the first of the hinterlands to be touched by the new subway system, it had accumulated enough population from Manhattan to make it worthwhile for Tammany to set it up as a subsidiary corporation. It meant there were that many more additional local government sinecures to be doled out as patronage. Its independence of Tammany remained nominal as long as the great Charles F. Murphy was leader of Tammany Hall, for Murphy named the Bronx leaders and told them what to do.

The real rival to old New York and Tammany in the area of political power was the Borough of Brooklyn, across the

East River, that occupied all of Kings County. In 1898 its population was mainly in the old City of Brooklyn—the present downtown section—with wealthy merchants and shipowners enjoying the peace and beauty of town houses on Brooklyn Heights.

There were other population centers such as Williamsburgh, Flatbush, Coney Island, Gravesend and New Utrecht, which had at various earlier stages enjoyed separate governmental identity as cities, towns or villages. They were separated from each other by miles of tomato and potato patches, through which one passed by trolley car. The population of the county as a whole was German, Scandinavian, Dutch and old colonial English, as opposed to the Irish, Jews and Italians who had assumed control in Manhattan. There were Irish Democratic politicians, of course, but Brooklyn voted Republican more often than not. In fact, in the first three presidential elections after consolidation, the county went Republican each time. At the third one, in 1908, its majority for William Howard Taft was big enough to throw the whole city into the Republican column.

The fourth borough in the 1898 package was Queens. Up to then, there had been a Queens County which took in all of the western third of Long Island except for the part occupied by Kings. The section nearest Manhattan, containing settlements and separate governments like Long Island City, Astoria and Flushing, totalling 114.7 square miles, kept the name Queens County and the additional identity as Queens Borough, when it was joined in the confederation. It was the biggest acquisition in terms of land area, but most of it was devoid of population. The rest of the original Queens County was newly renamed Nassau County and relegated to the status of exurbia.

# All the King's Horses

Both last and least was Richmond, the fifth borough, set up on the 70 square miles of hills and rills of Staten Island, duplicating the county of Richmond. It was utterly unconnected in interests with New York—too far across the waters of the harbor to serve, as the other boroughs rapidly did, as a bedroom for Manhattan's workers. Its villages and towns—Tottenville, Great Kills and Port Richmond, remained isolated and self-sufficient until the Verrazano Bridge of 1964 gave the island the first traffic link with the rest of the city. Cuddling geographically with New Jersey, Staten Island was part of New York State only because a sailing captain named Billop circumnavigated it by sloop within twenty-four hours, to win a dare of a royal colonial governor.

These were the elements out of which Greater New York was fashioned. Farseeing men of the time realized that eventually they would grow together anyhow, and that a unified government would serve the people best. Politically, the belief has lingered down through the years that Republican State Boss Thomas Platt, the United States Senator who controlled the Legislature, wanted the 320 square miles and the 3,500,000 people under one governmental roof because he saw possible advantages for his party. He thought, it is said, that the Republicans of Brooklyn and the handful of reasonably uncommitted voters in Queens and Richmond could give his party a chance to defeat Tammany Hall and elect a Mayor of the combined territory. If so, there probably never was a more mistaken long-range forecast. Brooklyn, as it developed, turned into the strongest Democratic voting unit in the United States.

Regardless of what Platt wanted, the people of Brooklyn, Queens and Richmond wanted no strong central government. To get consolidation through at all, its backers had to make concessions. The pound of flesh demanded and conceded amounted to this:

The new city would have a federal-type central government which Manhattan could not automatically dominate; independent local political organizations would be maintained, and there would be independent local governments dividing the powers with the city-wide government. Many of the guidelines for division of power were established at the very start in 1897, and others added in 1901.

The federal government was set up with a two house legislature that has lasted to this writing. The lower, most populous house was the Board of Aldermen, now the City Council, with the membership elected by districts roughly equal in population, within each borough, thus stressing both borough and locality identity. The senior body was the Board of Estimate and Apportionment, now the Board of Estimate, with eight members casting multiple weighted votes to accord with the confederation doctrine.

The Mayor, set up as the city executive, was given three votes in the Board of Estimate, as were the Controller and President of the Board of Aldermen, for a total of 9 out of 16 in the Board. The remainder was divided as follows: two votes each for the Borough Presidents of Manhattan and Brooklyn, in recognition of the larger populations they possessed, and one apiece for the Borough Presidents of The Bronx, Queens and Richmond. Years later, when Queens and The Bronx grew, they demanded equal voice in the Board, and in the reallocation, each Borough President was given two votes, for a total of ten. But the votes of the Mayor, Controller and President of the Council were increased to four each, thus retaining the principle that the city-wide elected officers should cast a majority, presumably for the city as against parochial interests.

Whether the city-wide officers had 9 out of 16, or 12 out of 22, the power to override Borough Presidential wishes was used little by any Mayor. He never knew when a split would occur among the Big Three, and he would need the vote of a couple of Borough Presidents to maintain a majority.

The Borough Presidents did nothing to discourage this consideration. With almost no prodding at all, they formed what amounted to a Borough Presidents' Union, one for all, and all for one.

In practice, it was not much different from the custom in the United States Senate of the body as a whole backing up any colleague on a matter important to him in his home state. Another accent on sectionalism within the body politic, was a custom that the three city-wide candidates should always be selected from separate boroughs, so that the place where a prospect for Mayor, Controller or Council President hangs his hat at night governs his chances as much as his stature and his ethnic background.

The scope of local government written into the 1898 and 1901 charters has been cut gradually. The extent to which it had existed can be told in the form of these examples:

Until Mayor Jimmy Walker established a city-wide Department of Sanitation, two of the five boroughs had their own street cleaners and snow shovellers, paid by the day whether they pushed or just leaned on their implements.

Until Fiorello H. La Guardia, in his first year as Mayor, made Robert Moses the overlord of a city Department of Parks, every borough had its own department, headed by its own commissioner.

## All the King's Horses

Until the major charter revision of 1937, every Borough President built all the public works in his borough, with his own engineers and with large laboring crews to back up private contract work.

Until the charter revision of 1961, every Borough President was the czar of his borough's streets and sewers. Even in Manhattan, it was the Borough President who decided what types of vehicles would be permitted on the West Side Highway and the East River Drive, built by *his* department, and whether the roadway needed repaving this year, or next.

Until the third Wagner administration set up a site-selection Board with a majority of its members named by the Mayor, any Borough President worth a hoot log-rolling in the Board of Estimate pretty much had the final say on the location of every schol, police station and fire house; whether he would accept a low-income housing project, or demand one instead for the middle-income family. This practice served to keep the civic worker interested as much in Borough Hall as in City Hall.

Then there were the five county governments, which no one was able to touch for decades, and which continue in existence today, partly as shadows, but also with substance. Prior to 1937 each county elected its own Sheriff, County Clerk and Register, with deputies and assistants galore, furnished by the local political machines. Today the Sheriff is a city-wide officer selected by Civil Service, and the duties of the County Clerk and Register are carried on within the court system, mostly out of patronage range.

But there still are six Surrogates, each elected locally, with tremendous legal patronage to dispense in the form of appointments of lawyers as guardians and referees. And there are five elected District Attorneys, the county Public Prosecutors, whose offices serve the local organizations well by being training grounds for young lawyers eager to get ahead in law, politics or government.

The right to nominate, the ability to elect all of these men who run wholly within a borough, or represent it city-wide, makes the party's county organization the responsible political unit, with nothing to match it on a city-wide basis. The state's election law, which mandates a kind of uniformity within the sixty-two separate counties of the state insofar as forming and running political organizations is concerned, fortifies the county as the unit, even when the county is within New York City.

As a result, a county chairman, while he may cooperate with the others, never accepts the idea that he can be bossed from without. He can be cut off from patronage at City Hall by a hostile Mayor, disregarded in state and federal jobs if he happens to be working at cross-purposes with the party's state organization, but as long as he has picked loyal friends for the local jobs, he is not in serious trouble.

The system has obvious disadvantages to those who like their politics to be neat and orderly, but it has its advantages, too. For example, it tends to limit the spread of corruption. As will be noted later, the Bronx District Attorney and the boss who directed his policies, barred racketeering from The Bronx when it was rife in Manhattan and tolerated in Kings. The 1941 deal which brought Frank S. Hogan in as New York County District Attorney and thus turned the office honest, could never have been effectuated on a city-wide basis.

In the key primary fights for the Democratic nomination for Mayor in 1925 and 1953, Manhattan and The Bronx, with intelligent leadership, fought for a needed change, while

Brooklyn, Queens and Richmond played a standpat game.

For good or for bad, there is an underlying sympathy on the part of the voter for the local concept. It may be of no concern to the mid-Manhattanite who came from Peoria and now works on Madison Avenue and lives on Sutton Place. But in the great sprawling areas to the north, south and east, the person with the plaint or the idea would rather deal with a Borough Hall than a City Hall, with a county political leader than a city-wide one. He has the feeling, right or wrong, that the local man knows his problem better, knows his neighborhood better.

As the power of the Borough Presidents has decreased, the people have learned to turn to their local Councilman. If some neighborhood never had a name of its own, or it got lost somehow over a century, the people dig up a name, and units like Cobble Hill and Strykers Bay suddenly appear. If the hearing on their problem is at City Hall, the Councilman, Assemblyman and State Senator had better be there, or face the wrath of the neighborhood-minded citizenry at the very next election.

It seems that the New Yorker may think of himself as an internationalist or a cosmopolite, but when it comes to his school set up, police protection or housing program, there is a sudden metamorphosis into the resident of Yorkville or Flatbush or one hundred other neighborhoods. Or, if the problem is larger, he speaks as the resident of Brooklyn or The Bronx or Queens or Richmond, even of Manhattan.

# 2. The Man in City Hall

Whoever is Mayor of New York is the biggest man in town, welcome everywhere. He is also the most picked upon —the man who gets the blame when *anything* goes wrong.

Those who have seen the job close-up have wondered why anybody would want to be Mayor, especially in recent years when the problems have multiplied in geometric progression. Yet there is never a dearth of candidates, especially if there is a chance of winning. The office represents the ultimate in municipal power and prestige, so men with ambition, especially those already involved in some phase of the city government, see it as their natural goal.

There are two legends of discouragement about the office of Mayor. One is that only mediocre men ever are elected to it. The second is that even if a well-qualified man wins, he seals his political tomb the day he enters City Hall. Neither proposition stands up.

From 1897, when the first man was picked for the office as it now exists, to the last Wagner administration ended in 1965, twelve different men were elected mayor, while two others held office briefly to fill vacancies. Of the elected dozen, eight were men of capacity. The list of them includes Seth Low, George B. McClellan, William J. Gaynor, John Purroy Mitchel, James J. Walker, Fiorello H. La Guardia, William O'Dwyer and Robert F. Wagner.

The theory that a mayor always kills himself off politically is based on the truth that no mayor has ever gone on to higher state or national office. But on the list of the qualified, only three ever had the desire to do so.

Of these three, two had no political party of state or national scope to support them. Mitchel was a Democrat, elected Mayor with Republican and independent citizens support, who was killed in an aviation training accident in World War I only months after he left office. La Guardia, nominally a Republican at the time of his first election, had been a political mugwump in Congress and was even more so as Mayor. He supported not a single Republican nominee for Governor, Senator or President during his twelve years in City Hall and the Republicans never thought they owed him promotion. The third on the list, Wagner, missed out not because he was Mayor or mugwump, but on the basis of poor timing—his major fault in many ways. With better judgment, he could have arranged for his own nomination on a winning ticket for Governor or Senator on any of several occasions in the years of his political power.

The office of Mayor abounds in power. The occupant is, or should be, the political leader of his party in the city, which extends to influence or dominate state party conventions.

While his patronage power is directly limited to some 500 jobholders out of 300,000 people whose salaries the city pays in whole or in part, the ones he can appoint are the men and women who run the city agencies and departments, who carry out policy. A word from the Mayor that a request from a friend be considered by an agency always gets respectful attention at the very least.

The Mayor also appoints judges of the lower courts, plums prized by the local political oranizations. The qualifications are not so high as to rule out most aspirants, and at the same time very able men can be put on the path to higher courts.

There are innumerable desirable places outside the area of routine patronage, like the unsalaried jobs as members of the Board of Education, the Board of Higher Education; part-time prestige posts on the City Planning Commission; and the dozens of committees which run Carnegie Hall, or the City Center, or raise money to beautify the streets or parks. Candidates for this kind of recognition, people who are endowed both with money and civic interest, press their friends to speak for them to the Mayor, and when the appointment is finally made, the winner and his supporters all owe the Mayor something.

The office of Mayor carries with it many creature comforts, to atone for the long hours, hard work and constant headaches. The salary is $50,000. With it goes a private limousine, available for pleasure as well as business, since the Mayor is always on duty. So are the chauffeurs, aides and police bodyguards. No Mayor worries about the chores of balancing his own checkbook, or buying his own plane tickets.

Public functions may be a chore, but when the Mayor goes to one—and he is always pressed to go—the red carpet is rolled out for him as if he were President of the United States. His attendance gives him a chance to do political fence-keeping as well as to catch up on things going on that his aides haven't told him about. In or out of City Hall, he is sought out for help, or offered advice, by the rich and influential, the poor and downtrodden. And when he really wants help or advice, his telephone call is never ignored.

Up to La Guardia's time, whoever was Mayor supplied his own home, distinguished officially only by the pair of police-station green lanterns hung outside the door. Since then, the city has supplied its Mayor with Gracie Mansion, containing the most charming interior of any old residence in the city, and located inside a park, with its lawn rolling down to the riverbank.

The headaches of the office are as impressive as the per-quisites. First, it is the biggest municipal housekeeping job in the world, with more garbage to collect, more streets to pave and police—just more of everything than exists any place else under a single governmental roof. Too often the solution of one problem means the creation of another, or its promotion to major status. And where the problems may not really be the Mayor's, there is a feeling of frustration because the public thinks they are his—that he does supervise everything in the city and can command the ideas, money and manpower to overcome any difficulty.

There are many areas of paramount importance in which the Mayor figures only because of the prestige of his office, rather than by law. Frequently, he has been deliberately ex-cluded by statute, because the public thought, originally, it wanted politics eliminated.

For example, education. The school system is paid for by the city, with a partial rebate from the state. The Mayor names the unsalaried members of the Board of Education to head up the school system, and the public assumes that he directs, through them, the way the schools are to be run. In actuality, even the Board of Education doesn't run the school system. The Board itself floats uneasily on a sea of civil service administrators, statutorily protected in office. The school system is a giant bureaucracy that may be influenced by the Mayor, but not ordered about.

Consider the subways. The courts and the legislature adopted the fiction decades ago that transportation, like education, was a matter of broad concern to be protected by the state from local canoodling. The current agency set up by state law to run the subway system is a three-man authority, created in 1953, to which the Mayor names one member, the Governor a second, and Albany and City Hall negotiate for the third.

Housing the under-salaried is by law the job of the New York City Housing Authority, to which the Mayor names the members, but its rules and practices are dominated by the guidebooks of the state and federal agencies which supply most of the funds. In any event, it is independent of the Mayor, the book says. But let there be a rat in a school, a crime in the subway, or a family dispossessed, and everyone will come arunnin' to City all to demand corrective action by the Mayor.

The Mayor can influence action, even where he can't order it, if city money is a factor. An agency created by law to be independent of the Mayor stays that way just so long as it uses only its own money and never has to go to City Hall for an appropriation.

A classic example of the truly independent agency is the Tri-Borough Bridge and Tunnel Authority, which runs the city's toll bridges and tunnels. Its members are appointed by the Mayor, and theoretically removable by him for cause, but he never gets a chance to know what is going on inside. As long as the dimes, quarters and half dollars roll in, it can, and sometimes does, thumb its nose at City Hall. Its franchise was never supposed to be irrevocable, but contracts it made with bondholders have had that effect.

In the places where the mayor's control is clear, it is the grasp of the purse strings that makes him the boss that he really is. He prepares for all city departments the annual expense budget, which lists every job and sets every salary. Others may do the spade work on the capital budget, which contains appropriations of borrowed money for public improvements, but everything the Mayor wants is in it, and nothing more. In theory, the Board of Estimate and City Council can overrule him on both expense and capital budgets, but they don't. After all, he takes the rap for the taxes, and no one seeks to share that privilege.

His power over money influences policy and projects outside of government. A Lincoln Center, though built basically with private funds, needs city help for site assemblage and the write-down of land costs. A Wollman skating rink in Central Park, or a Shakespeare company touring the schools needs city money. A hospital short of housing for its nursing and intern staffs counts on a loan from the city's little FHA, the Mitchell-Lama housing operation. The sponsors of each and every one go first to City Hall for the go-ahead signal before even approaching the agency nominally in charge.

The Mayor who keeps his door and his ears open for the important people builds up a reservoir of good will, a credit to be drawn upon at election time, or time of other crisis. The newspaper publisher whose pet project is just about to get off the ground with the help of city money finds himself editorially less vehement even if he joins the usual election-year drive against higher city budgets. In this, he is not much different from the family on home relief.

The responsibility for money is both a blessing and a burden to the Mayor in dealing with the city's Civil Service employees. Traditionally, the rank and file, while protected in tenure by the Civil Service laws, still courted the Mayor for extras. The well-organized blocs like police, firemen and sanitation men could count on a steady flow of additional benefits in return for political support. Individuals in any department fared better in assignments or in getting merit raises, if they were active election district captains. The rest could usually be counted on to vote for the incumbent, anyhow, on the simple theory that the devil they knew was better than the devil they didn't.

The situation changed, but not necessarily for the Mayor's benefit. The Wagner administration gave the employees a career and salary plan, and collective bargaining rights which, together, generate mass pressures for ever-new benefits and pay raises. Instead of removing pressures from the Mayor, the programs have increased them, but with less assurance that what they have won en masse will be registered appreciatively at the polls.

For the higher echelons of public service, there are lots of candidates. Unfortunately, most of those who are willing to run a city department aren't able. Jim Farley, as patronage dispenser for the incoming Roosevelt national administration, had an eye-opening experience that winter of 1932 through 1933. He had no idea what positions in the federal service were best for the grafter or empire builder until he canvassed the lists of applicants and saw the lineup of the wrong kind of people for a particular post. Fortunately, there was a depression on which made government jobs attractive to qualified people, too.

A mayor about to take office, and wanting to run a creditable administration, may very well find that able selfless administrators, knowledgeable and technically qualified, willing to take a job without tenure, are in short supply. When the author covered City Hall in the Walker administration, the requirements were not so high. Every commissioner was a district leader, except a handful that were in office because they were personal friends of the Mayor. Some were competent, but that wasn't the requirement.

Since La Guardia's time, and the increase in problems as well as public standards of service, no mayor has tried to run the city with purely political selections. His party may be able to recommend to him a highly qualified Hospitals, Health or Traffic Commissioner, but the chances are that he will have to canvass the country, and raise the pay, to get a good man.

The Police Commissioner he picks must know police work, be expert at public relations, sound on civil rights, and combine loyalty to the Mayor with a hide like an elephant's. That is why to be a good mayor, the man in City Hall must have a wide knowledge of manpower sources to tap for his top jobs. La Guardia's Congress background gave him knowledge of able federal people he could draft into city service. O'Dwyer knew the city and everybody who was anybody in it. Wagner used a network of friends and associates he had more or less inherited from his father.

For the lesser jobs, men and women noted more for political, fraternal or ethnic group activity than for fitness for government have continued to seek office and to be appointed.

From them the Mayor must be ready to run, if necessary. For example, La Guardia is often recalled for his remark that "when I make a mistake, it's a beaut."

He had named to a lower court bench a sympathizer with the anti-Semitic, isolationist Christian Front, hoping to placate some of that group in an election year. The Mayor knew exactly what he was doing. When the appointment bounced back at him, he had his alibi—quoted above—all ready and he capitalized on it.

The growth of the Mayor's personal staff at City Hall has kept pace with the work load. In Walker's time, four were enough to carry the ball on policy, with a handful of clerks for the routine, and some drones just on the payroll. La Guardia borrowed aides and clerks right and left from the city departments, without bothering to shift them to the City Hall payroll. O'Dwyer and Impellitteri did the same.

Wagner, taking office, found 17 of these waifs whom he shifted from the payrolls of departments they never saw to that of City Hall itself. With the new agencies and activities that came into being in his time, he wound up with 84 men and women in City Hall and 73 more in the office of the City Administrator. This office was created in 1954 as a sop to civic groups clamoring for efficiency via the city manager route.

The Mayor, who is an ex-officio member of countless city boards and commissions, but never sits on them, once was required to attend every meeting of the city's real governing board, the Board of Estimate, or forfeit for the day the three votes he cast in it. La Guardia changed this with the creation of the office of Deputy Mayor, under the 1937 charter. By 1965 the Mayor had three deputy mayors, as well as a dozen aides with the titles of Assistants to the Mayor. The deputy mayors, the assistants, are all charged with the task of doing what the Mayor would do, if he had time.

So no matter how important anyone of these may be, it is the Mayor he is working for, not himself. He is helping the Mayor leave that very different stamp on the office, and on the city itself, which distinguishes each administration so completely from another.

The mayors this author has known well were Walker, O'Brien, La Guardia, O'Dwyer, Impellitteri and Wagner. Closeups of each follow:

## WALKER

Jimmy Walker combined personal charm and quickness of wit to a degree rarely seen in public office or elsewhere. He was usually elsewhere. A gay, handsome fashion-plate, he preferred the café society of the speakeasy age to duller political company. Since he seldom rose before noon, City Hall saw him possibly a dozen hours a week.

Anywhere he was, he was always the consummate actor who could turn resentment to affection with just a grin or a wink; could win a lifelong admirer with a smile and a hand wave. Gestures were his substitute for finishing a sentence or rounding out a phrase, but he never had any trouble communicating with a crowd, whether it was watching him lead up Fifth Avenue a parade demanding legalized beer, or disposing of an accumulation of city affairs on a Board of Estimate calendar.

In City Hall a problem could hang fire for months, finally reaching the last deadline for settlement. Walker would start out of his private office, annexing an aide or expert on the problem as he went through the door. The briefing lasted as long as it took the two of them to mount the single flight of stairs to the Board of Estimate Chamber, with Walker digesting every morsel that could be crammed in en route. By the time he took his seat, he had the solution that would be city policy. After he uttered it, he never gave it another thought. He learned only by ear, and what he learned, having passed through his agile mind on the way to the vocal cords, was transmitted into the action of the day. It is astounding, in retrospect just as it was at the time, how much he could get done that way, how much city progress followed his waves of the magic wand.

His term and a half in office produced the city's first Hospitals Department and city-wide sanitation system. He started the West Side Highway. New York Central freight trains blighted the whole West Side as they ran at street level on Tenth, Eleventh and Twelfth avenues, presenting a problem no administration had been able to resolve. He worked out a deal with the railroad, which put the tracks underground in some areas, elevated between the blocks in others.

In faraway European shipyards, giant ocean liners were being built, too long for the longest city piers to accommodate. The Hoover administration's War Department wouldn't let the city extend its longest ones further into the Hudson. Jimmy made room for the not-yet-completed Normandie, Bremen, Rex and their successors, by cutting inshore the needed number of feet, so that the ship prows rose and sank with the tides where Manhattan rock had been.

He laid the groundwork for the Tri-Borough Bridge, the Queens-Midtown Tunnel, and hundreds of miles of new subways, not built until the WPA and the PWA arrived with federal funds in the La Guardia era. He even put into effect a program of paying for subway construction out of the money coming from the then annual increase in real estate assessments.

What ruined Jimmy was his complete amorality in the fields of money and sex. To protect him against himself, even before he took office, a group of friends took up a quiet collection and packed off his steady girl of the day, with a bundle of cash and a request she never come back. Jimmy shrugged and found himself another, with no trouble at all. During his first year as Mayor, the Catholic Church tried similarly to intervene.

An eminent layman, representing himself as coming from the Cardinal, lectured Jimmy that he was bringing shame on his wife and on the church of which he was nominally a member.

Jimmy teetered characteristically back and forth on his toes, and naming two well-known churchgoers whose private morals were no better than his own, said:

"You go back and tell the Cardinal to take care of his two altar boys and I'll take care of myself."

The church bided its time for six years. Then Jimmy got into trouble over money he had taken and couldn't explain convincingly, and he resigned as Mayor just one jump ahead of probable removal by the Governor. When he quit, he planned to run again for Mayor to fill the vacancy caused by his own resignation. If elected, this would be vindication by the voters which would legally as well as practically, absolve him of past sins. He had the approval of the Democratic bosses, Curry and McCooey, for the program. No sooner was he out, temporarily, when the Church struck.

## The Man in City Hall

It picked the funeral of a Tammany brave as the spot for a representative of the Cardinal to delivery a eulogy of the departed, noting pointedly that the latter had never shamed his wife by consorting with other women, and had never been accused of taking a gratuity for a favor. As the Church spoke, Curry and McCooey listened. And just to make sure that the public got the message, trusted newsmen were tipped off to the significance. The unique reign of Walker was ended.

## O'Brien

John P. O'Brien was picked by Curry to run for Mayor in Walker's place because he was so different. In this, the choice was 100 percent successful.

To the degree that Walker was quick-witted, O'Brien was slow. Jimmy had a girl in every port, O'Brien went home at night to his wife and nine children. Jimmy, who loved the spotlight, held it all his life; O'Brien was a New York County Surrogate obscured even in his own court by the brilliance of the other Surrogate, James A. Foley. Walker gave orders —took them from no one; O'Brien was a good organization man who waited until he heard from Tammany.

O'Brien's everyday decisions were made for him by a Tammany war board, set up to meet the political and governmental problems created by the depression and the Seabury investigation. There were some smart men on it, like Samuel Untermyer, Max Steuer and John H. Delaney, but the limited viewpoint of Curry and others prevailed, so that most of the orders to City Hall from uptown merely compounded prior errors.

The Mayor's dependence on the political leaders for action

or tutelage was never more widely advertised than by the occasion he was asked, at City Hall, who his new police commissioner would be. Using a phrase common in politics, but rare as coming from the nominal appointing power, O'Brien said:

"I haven't had the word yet."

Reporters racing for telephones to their city desks corrupted the answer so that in print it read:

"I haven't heard yet."

For this he is remembered in political lore by those who remember him at all.

## La Guardia

Fiorello H. La Guardia was alternately a little boy chasing fire engines or leading a symphony orchestra, and a devoted Mayor trying to give the people the most for their money. His tantrums, often genuine, were the noisiest in town, for he was determined not to be second best in anything. For the first eight of his twelve years in City Hall, he was the best Mayor the city had ever seen. In his last term his heart and interests were so much involved in the winning of World War II that he paid scant attention to the daily chores.

Though he always pretended complete independence of political considerations, he had a political awareness as keen as any man who ever held public office, most often scorning formal party ties while building a personal political machine. At various times in his career he ran as a Republican, a Progressive and a Socialist. His final enrollment was in the American Labor party. In 1938, he promised he would be Thomas E. Dewey's New York City campaign manager when the

latter ran for Governor, and he wound up leaking word to
the press that he favored Lehman's reelection. In 1944, he
ruined a Republican candidate for Senator with just one quip.
Asked by the press whether he favored Republican Secretary
of State Thomas J. Curran, a onetime Alderman, or Robert
F. Wagner, Sr., the Democratic incumbent, La Guardia wrote
on a piece of paper: "Curran, a good Alderman; Wagner, a
good Senator."

Before he became Mayor, his record was as varied as he
was—personally and politically unpredictable.

He served in Congress as a Republican before World War
I and retained his seat in the House while flying as a com-
missioned officer with the infant Army Air Force on the
Italian front. Years later in City Hall, he markedly preferred
the title Major to Mayor. As the result of a 1919 city election in an off-year for the Democrats, he spent two undis-
tinguished and quarrelsome years of the Hylan administration
as President of the old Board of Aldermen.

After that he went back to Congress from a new Harlem
district and rapidly became New York's member of the Nor-
ris bloc of Western progressive Republicans derided by the
Old Guard as "sons of the wild jackass." These were the years
when the local Republicans would deny him their nomination
on occasion, and he would win anyhow, because he was as
hardworking a Congressman as the House contained, servic-
ing his own district as well as serving the nation.

When he ran for Mayor against Jimmy Walker in 1929
he lost by the record majority of 498,000. But he kept his
seat in Congress until the 1932 Roosevelt landslide, when even
*he* couldn't survive on the Republican ticket, though he was
at the height of his congressional repute. In 1933, defeated

Republican congressmen were a dime a dozen, except La Guardia. Samuel Seabury, riding the wave of civic prestige as the man who revealed Tammany's corruption and made it vulnerable to defeat, wanted no one but La Guardia to run for Mayor.

Seabury felt La Guardia's personal honesty met the paramount requirement of the day. Most of the Republican leaders wanted General John F. O'Ryan of World War I renown. What followed amused insiders. Republican State Chairman W. Kingsland Macy, supporting Seabury's view, packed overnight the so-called Republican Committee of 100 with 200 added La Guardia boosters. O'Ryan withdrew and the winning Republican-Fusion ticket emerged.

La Guardia paid off his debt to the nonpolitical O'Ryan by making him Police Commissioner but denounced Macy the first opportunity he could create. He wanted no political IOU's to the Republican pros in circulation.

When he took office as Mayor, the city had no place to go but up from the financial and spiritual depths to which it had sunk with the depression and Tammany. La Guardia, bustling and colorful, made City Hall the busiest place in town. He was public relations conscious to the $n$th degree. For example, when he was tipped off that big-shot underworld jailbirds were living it up with parties and women in the city prison, he didn't show his hand by firing the Tammany warden—he staged a raid at dawn with reporters and cameramen, who didn't know until they got there what the assignment was about. They were news-happy with a story that just wrote itself.

When he wanted to build up sentiment for a New York City airport, he focussed attention by refusing to get off his commercial transport plane at Newark—the regular stop then serving New York—pointing out that his ticket called for the company to take him to New York. They did, too.

He worked hand in glove with Roosevelt's New Deal in Washington, commuting to the capital to bring back funds for things like the completion of the Tri-Borough Bridge, subway cars to use in the new Independent subway, money for jobs, for housing, for parks and playgrounds. He had the political courage to put into effect a city sales tax to finance home relief, even though he had helped lick a federal sales tax in Congress a scant two years before. From the point of view of revenue, public acceptance and ease of administration, his sales tax was the best in the country for years thereafter.

Seabury was correct in that no one ever had to question La Guardia's honesty when it came to money matters. Intellectually, he was often a downright faker. When he ran in 1929, he was nominated for Mayor by a city convention of typical Republican ward heelers. He brought them to their feet, cheering, by telling them that when he was elected, they would get the patronage jobs. Four years later, with professional politicians in disrepute, he screamed that he would permit no "clubhouse loafers" on the public payroll.

One of his facets was that he distrusted people who became his friends after he was Mayor—on the theory that they were cultivating him just to get something—and he would toss them to the wolves if the occasion demanded. But he never went back on old friends. There were two Tammany district leaders who had always refrained from stealing votes from La Guardia when he ran for Congress, a forbearance he appreciated. When he was Mayor and they got into trouble, Fiorello soft-pedalled it.

He made many fine appointments to public office and usually set high standards of municipal service, yet he named

# The Man in City Hall

Democratic mediocrities to the bench simply because they had served with him in Congress.

His moods were myriad and he indulged them at City Hall, at his favorite hangout for cocktail conferences, the Engineers' Club, or at his apartment on the fringes of Harlem. Working uptown one Sunday afternoon, his concentration was thrown off by the noise of bombs exploded by marchers in an Italian church parade. He called the local precinct and ordered the parade broken up by the police. The captain in charge sent out an SOS for Vito Marcantonio, the Mayor's protégé and successor as padrone of the Italian Harlem community. Marc called the Mayor, to be met with a tirade about the bombs.

"But you can't have an Italian parade without bombs," remonstrated Marc. "You should know, you've led this same parade yourself every year up to this."

"All right," said Fiorello weakening, "just one more bomb."

The parade continued, with bombs, unmolested.

La Guardia, long on imagination, was also a fiend for getting the things he wanted carried out. So the city got its World's Fair in 1939, a High School of Science and of Music and Art, its New York City Center, decades ahead of the cultural explosion of the 1960's. He just never got around to the beer gardens along the Harlem, which he dreamed of as New York's answer to the Paris sidewalk café.

There were two things, beyond his control, that he never got. One was the Democratic nomination for the United States Senate, which never came close, no matter how much he courted Franklin D. Roosevelt and Roosevelt's New York political agent, Bronx boss Flynn. The second was the commission as Brigadier General in the army in World War II. Roosevelt did send the proposed nomination to the War Department, but Secretary of War Henry L. Stimson, and Chief of Staff General George Marshall stood firm. They wanted no political generals, particularly a La Guardia with the campaign in Italy coming up.

When La Guardia left the Mayor's chair, he did so disappointed, bitter and also a sick man. By mid-summer 1945, the war in Europe was over and La Guardia, though he never said so publicly, would have welcomed the chance at a fourth term as Mayor. He had no place else to go. When the Republicans and the newly formed Liberal party, the leadership of both of which he had antagonized, indicated they would not support him, he made sure they couldn't elect anyone else. He induced his long-term ally, Newbold Morris, to run for Mayor independently, creating a three-way race and doubly insuring the election of William O'Dwyer on the Democratic ticket.

## O'DWYER

William O'Dwyer seemed to have everything in his favor that a mayor needs for the job: a quick mind, intimate knowledge of his city, willingness to work, charm and political sophistication. At the end of his first two years in office, two dozen of the city's most influential civic associations joined at a public dinner in paying tribute to his successful carrying on of the city's business in the trying postwar years. At the end of his first term, he was reelected with the greatest of ease.

Yet he appeared to those who watched closely to fit Churchill's description of Stalin's Russia—"a riddle wrapped in a mystery, inside an enigma."

Even when he seemed most sure of himself, he acted as if he was afraid to be Mayor. Under the election law, a man nominated for office at a primary election can not withdraw unless later on he is picked for an office filled by a state or judicial district convention. The day O'Dwyer was nominated at the primary in 1945, he privately suggested a judicial nomination for himself as an out. After four years in office, with reelection almost certain, he declined to run for a second term. This is a gambit which normally calls for a draft movement, to which the candidate will "reluctantly" yield. In O'Dwyer's script, the draft movement started, finished, and he still said "no." He even pushed others into the picture to succeed himself. Only a last-minute midnight conference at Gracie Mansion, at which Ed Flynn brought real pressure, produced O'Dwyer's final consent.

Reelected, he spent a brief period in a hospital recuperating from the flu. While there he quietly filed his retirement papers, to eliminate himself from the office to which he had just been reelected. His longtime associate, Jim Moran, who acted as though he owned O'Dwyer, retrieved the papers from the retirement board, brought them to the hospital room, and burned them in O'Dwyer's presence.

Moran tarnished the considerable accomplishments of the O'Dwyer administration by a later conviction for graft. He used a job O'Dwyer had given him in the Fire Department to levy tribute on businesses subject to Fire Department permits and inspection. When prosecutors and investigators offered Moran inducements to involve "others," his reply uniformly was, "I was born a man and I'll die a man." He spent seven years in prison and emerged with his lips still closed.

O'Dwyer, not even under fire at the time, nevertheless resigned as Mayor long before Moran got into trouble, or police graft was unveiled. He conceived the idea he would be happy in Mexico, as the U. S. Ambassador, and persuaded Flynn, as National Committeeman, to ask the favor of President Harry S. Truman.

Truman, who carried a grudge well, had one against O'Dwyer because of the position the latter took, in 1948, that Truman should be dumped because he couldn't possibly be elected. But Flynn persuaded Truman, as a good party man, that the Democrats would have a better chance of electing a governor in 1950 if a special contest for mayor was waged simultaneously. O'Dwyer got his ambassadorship, but the rest of the program flopped. The Democrats lost both the governorship and the mayoralty.

O'Dwyer's ambivalence showed in other ways. He had accumulated prestige as a crusading District Attorney in Brooklyn, but it turned out later that he had clamped the investigative lid on at least one explosive situation. As Mayor he railed publicly at the control of Tammany Hall by the underworld but privately he worked with the status quo. He ruled out interference in the Police Department by other politicians but tolerated graft-taking from bookmakers by the police brass.

He followed the La Guardia tradition to the extent of appointing a substantial number of competent office holders. He increased, rather than cut off, the assignments and prestige enjoyed by Robert Moses in the La Guardia administration. He rushed school and housing construction programs. He had the political courage to raise the subway fare from the sacrosanct nickel to a dime to meet inflated costs.

New York liked "Bill-O" and his blarney, and most people gave up trying to find out what made him tick. He, in turn, was in love with the city in which he had grown up, where an immigrant could rise to become the Mayor. When the Mexican adventure was over, he came back here to live because he liked it here, and also so that he could throw the lie into the teeth of those who whispered that he was afraid to come back. He never was involved thereafter in politics and by the time of his death, had been out of the picture for several years.

## IMPELLITTERI

When Vincent Impellitteri's name was announced in 1945 as the Democratic-American Labor party choice for President of the City Council, junking a previously prepared ticket, there was wonderment why the two parties had come up with this obscure Clerk to a State Supreme Court Justice. Bert Stand, the quick-witted puckish Secretary of Tammany Hall, told reporters that they had needed a Manhattan Italian for the ticket and had found Impellitteri's name in the Green Book, the pocket-size annual directory of city departments and office holders.

Stand knew better, of course (*see Chapter 8*) but his was the only explanation in town at the time and many accepted it. Things like that had happened before, though never for a job so high-ranking that it carried with it succession to the mayoralty if the mayor died or resigned or was removed.

When O'Dwyer did resign five years later, Impellitteri became Acting Mayor and aspired to hold the job in his own right. At first glance he had little chance. Carmine De Sapio, leader of Tammany Hall, and Ed Flynn already had an agreement with the Liberal party to name Ferdinand Pecora, who had won fame years before with his Wall Street investigation. The Republicans had to have a candidate of their own, since it was a gubernatorial election year as well. So Impellitteri announced he would run independently, and he did. He was the first man ever to win a major office in New York City without the nomination of a previously established political party. He put together a one-time-only ragtag and bobtail outfit called the Experience party.

He had a number of things going for him. He had inherited O'Dwyer's very competent and imaginative press secretary. A suggestion that Impellitteri could assure himself a place on the Supreme Court bench was turned by this secretary into a "half a million dollar bribe," this being the computed value of the bench salary for the full term of fourteen years, with no allowance for taxes.

Secondly, he was projected as the man with the experience in the job, though in essence it was limited to attending public dinners and Board of Estimate meetings. He also won the endorsement of Robert Moses, still functioning under him as the grand pooh-bah of planning and projects.

Thirdly, he had a specialized religious appeal as the only Catholic of the three major candidates, Pecora, and Corsi the Republican, being Protestants.

Fourth, Pecora, softened by many years on the bench, was anything but the fighting candidate he would have been a dozen years before.

Finally, his name, too long for newspaper headlines, was shortened by the newspapers to "Impy," and the nickname, projecting even further the idea of an independent who spurned the bosses and their gold, caught the public's fancy. He won with ease, getting 1,161,000 votes to 935,000 for Pecora and 382,000 for Corsi.

If the public thought it was electing a genuine independent, it was rapidly disabused. His first move was to appoint a former leader of Tammany Hall as his patronage secretary, with a free hand to deal with jobs. He courted all the leaders who had opposed him, except De Sapio, with whom he carried on an inconclusive grudge fight the whole three years he held office.

Inside City Hall, he showed not much more capacity for the job than the previous interim Mayor, O'Brien, and turned over the business of running the city to Moses and to his Budget Director. It was said at the time that he closed his door to all others to keep the problems out. But no Mayor can really do that, so Impy wrestled as best he could with a city financial crisis, which produced another increase in the subway fare, to 15 cents, and an economy drive which cut down popular projects. He simultaneously got the blame for a temporary rent-control fiasco. By the summer of 1953, when he sought nomination for reelection in the Democratic primary, his public appeal had worn very thin.

While Robert F. Wagner, Jr., then Borough President of Manhattan, ran as a theoretical underdog against him in the primary, Wagner won by a margin of nearly two to one.

Impy was then still under fifty-five years of age, too young for a city pension, and out of a job. But sentiment came to his rescue. The other members of the Board of Estimate on which Wagner and Impellitteri had served—including reformer Rudolph Halley—asked Wagner to appoint Impellitteri to a lower court judgeship. Wagner agreed, provided they would urge it publicly, and no political deals were involved.

The new Mayor exploded, with rare fury, when on the day he took office, with a commitment to Impy, he found that the outgoing Mayor had parcelled out four jobs, two to his own and two to Wagner supporters, which made the whole thing look like a trade. He appointed Impy anyhow, and the latter served for several years after his pension rights had matured.

## WAGNER

Robert Ferdinand Wagner, Jr., who served three terms as New York's Mayor, was born and reared to practice the art and science of government. From boyhood, he was steeped in politics and statecraft by a famous father who acted as political tutor for junior. The senior Wagner, whose name was later a household word, made his first major imprint on government as co-chairman, with young Alfred E. Smith, of the factory investigating committee which was the legislative aftermath of the famous Triangle Shirtwaist Company fire of 1911.

The reforms which stemmed from its report put New York ahead of every other state of the Union in the area of social progress and concern. From legislative leadership in Albany, the senior Wagner went to the state court bench and from there, in 1926, to the United States Senate. In Washington his name went on legislation in the fields of labor, housing and finance which became the backbone of the Roosevelt New Deal in the years from 1933 to 1945.

The elder Wagner could have been Mayor. He turned down in 1925 Al Smith's plea that he be the candidate against Mayor John F. Hylan and Jimmy Walker won the nod only as second choice. All through his life he and his cronies, the greats of politics of the era, not only regarded politics as a business but as a hobby. The Smiths, Foleys, Walkers and Wagners talked politics whenever they got together, and frequently a silent listener in the room was the widowed Senator's only son, Robert F. Wagner, Jr.

The young man learned politics from the war-horses' mouths, as they chewed over things that had happened, why they happened, and how other things could be made to happen, in the broad scene of government and politics. Young Bob was endowed with a fine memory which developed later into a total "recall" of events, conversations and commitments of weeks, months and years before.

Training in listening without interrupting served him well, too, in his later role as presiding officer at long drawn-out public hearings at which every speaker, repetitive as he might be, nevertheless received attention from the Mayor.

Young Wagner inherited from his father a social consciousness tied in intimately with the political scene and also social welfare connections valuable for information, prestige and even campaign contributions. Less fortunately, he inherited also his father's views on when to move and when to avoid action, or postpone it. For example, his father worked on the theory that if only two courses of political action seemed open—both unpleasant—the whole mess might resolve itself if he just waited it out. Also, that it was good politics as well as good government to bring potentially adverse interests into the conference room, and make them participants in working out the solution or details, thus binding them to support things they might otherwise have balked at.

Mayor Wagner was so committed to both these approaches of his father that no one was ever able to win an argument with him on the opposing thesis that immediate action, even if not the best considered, was sometimes preferable to delay. The net result was that with newspapers always committed to clamoring for action, his three administrations had a bad press.

# The Man in City Hall

An exception was when the Mayor moved in to settle the prolonged newspaper strike in the winter of 1962, which lasted to the early part of 1963. The publishers, who had been reading and believing their own editorial writers' appraisals of the Mayor, were amazed at Wagner's exhibition of capacity, sagacity and endurance. For nearly a year thereafter, the editorial tone was different.

Those who thought Wagner wishy-washy, unable to make up his mind, were far from the truth, but the blame for the error was not entirely theirs. Wagner knew instinctively what he would have to do, and would do. If he didn't like the prospect, he stalled, claiming he hadn't made up his mind—was still weighing the values. An illustration:

> Two men close to him were vying for appointment as Corporation Counsel. Both were qualified, and both were men to whom the Mayor was obligated. A third aide unintentionally mentioned the subject, and the Mayor said he hadn't made up his mind. The uninvolved assistant said:
>
> "Bob, I don't really want to know which one will get it, but please don't insult my intelligence by telling me you don't know. What you mean is that you haven't figured out yet how to break the news to the loser."

The Mayor had the grace to blush.

Again, seeking the concensus approach, the Mayor would devise or accept a program, and persuade someone on the outside to beat the drums for it before he broached it himself. He made himself appear as a man who had been forced or persuaded to do something he had planned from the start.

His tactics thus served to dull the shine of three outstanding terms in City Hall. In the field of money honesty, he was as untouchable as La Guardia. In terms of meeting the problems of the day—far greater than those existing in the La Guardia era, which were big enough—he did even better than the Little Flower. Action in the fields of police, education, housing, hospitals, health, traffic and civil rights—to cite only a few— were on a broader scale and with better administration and results. The Wagner middle-income housing program was the best in the nation, but he allowed two obscure legislators to garner the credit for it. La Guardia would have blazoned it on and from the rooftops. La Guardia got credit as an innovator, Wagner always looked like the reluctant dragon.

Fortunately for Wagner, as a candidate he had an uncanny sense of identification with the common man. The walking-tour type of campaign was made for him. As he went through some crowded neighborhood on foot he knew just what the "little schnook" on the street was thinking about. Somehow the little schnook knew he knew, and voted for him.

He made the same sharp evaluation of the capacity of his staff, and used the members accordingly.

One important aide, at the very start of the Wagner regime, said to another of almost equal rank:

"While he's in, he will use you, and me, and everyone else, as he needs us, no more, no less, and he will always be the Mayor."

The remark was 100 percent accurate. Also, he staffed the city service at the top level with men and women who were always at least qualified, and in many instances outstanding. Partisan politics figured very little in these posts.

As Mayor-elect, he woke up to the fact that almost every one of his scheduled assistants in City Hall was Jewish. To his credit, he did not cancel a single assignment, but a broader balance was presented in the press by timing each staff announcement with an important non-Jewish administration nomination. Eventually the staff expansion and attrition resulted in representation of every race and creed.

Wagner had climbed the governmental ladder, with parental assistance, from his first post as Assemblyman, to Tax Commissioner, to Building Commissioner, to Chairman of the City Planning Commission. In the latter post, and also as Borough President and Mayor, he cultivated the New York Establishment, from social workers and labor leaders to big businessmen and philanthropists, giving time, interest and sympathy to their causes. Eventually they all felt that they had a stake in keeping him in office.

His actions turned out to be prescient, for when he broke with the party organizations in 1961, it was the social workers and labor leaders who provided the manpower, and the philanthropists the money and prestige, to fashion the all-important primary election victory over the machines.

But just as Wagner was good as a Mayor, so was he a failure at the task of being the leader of his party. He didn't work at it, nor did he permit anyone else to take over. He seemed to prefer a vacuum into which he could move when, and only when, it suited him.

When Robert F. Kennedy decided he could establish a political base in New York by running for United States Senator, he checked first with the Mayor. Wagner made it clear that the move was okay with him, provided Kennedy declared publicly that he wouldn't have come in without his permission. Kennedy issued the proper statements, the Mayor confirmed them but the nuance was lost on the newspapers and on the public, because Wagner had never acted enough like a boss for anyone to believe that he was.

Speaking of bosses, the Mayor was loath originally to dump Carmine G. De Sapio, supporter and good leader of Tammany Hall. But the reform movement in the Democratic party had so smeared the De Sapio name that his support at the polls was becoming a liability. Wagner, reading the signs and dedicated like any other politician to the preservation of his own career, shrugged his shoulders and allied himself with the ouster movement.

In his final term as Mayor his chief political adviser and supporter was not just any Democratic party figure, but Alex Rose, veteran leader of the Liberal party. When Wagner declined to consider a fourth term as Mayor, Rose and his party fused with the Republicans behind John V. Lindsay. Naturally, Lindsay campaigned against what had gone on before and promised to do better. Abe Beame, with whom the Mayor had split earlier, owed Wagner nothing. As the Democratic nominee for Mayor, Beame ran on his own record as Controller. Since no one ran on the Wagner record, everyone ran away from it. The Mayor's mañana attitude also left the city in a financial hole. Thus his twelve years in City Hall came to an end, not with a bang but a whimper.

No one took seriously Wagner's hope, born before he left City Hall, and nurtured by him in the months following, that he would emerge as the Democratic-Liberal candidate for Governor in 1966. His belated and grudging support of the eventual Democratic nominee was the most public evidence of his disappointment.

# 3. The Parties

Political parties operated in New York under a law passed in 1911 to meet the demands of reformers of that era for a direct primary system that would take the control of party nominations out of the hands of the political bosses. Though amended hundreds of times, the law retained its basic premise that while the political poker game was open to all, the rules should make it harder for the amateurs and penny-ante-addicts to play. This was hardly surprising since the rules were drawn up, and amended when necessary, by the professionals within both parties.

This statewide law covered the operations of the parties for the nomination and election of those who ran statewide, such as Governors, Senators or presidential electors, and also for those who ran in New York City alone. The terms were different, however. It was difficult for voters to band together to nominate a candidate for statewide office other than as a nominee of one of the two major parties. Even the highly organized Communists, in the 1940's, needed help, and got it, from the Republicans on one occasion. On the other hand, when it came to elections for Mayor or other local offices, independents were able to get on the ballot with relative ease, and having gotten on, won the election itself. Nothing of the kind ever happened in a race for statewide office, under the statewide rules.*

The party enrollments in New York City over the years showed that the Democrats sometimes outnumbered their principal opposition, the Republicans, by as much as 4 to 1, and never less than 5 to 2. They consistently had from two-thirds to three-quarters of the total enrollment in all parties. Allowing for those who signified Democratic leanings because they had vague ideas it would help them out of traffic tickets or jury service, the cold figures still showed a Democratic edge so substantial that the party should never have lost an election. The record books told a different story.

From 1930 through 1965 there were nine regular and two special elections for Mayor, out of which the Democrats won six and lost five. In three special elections for other city-wide office, they won one by a landslide, squeaked through in another, and lost a third.†

The record was not much more impressive in the city vote for the Democratic nominees for state and national office. The

---

* To nominate a candidate for Governor, or a slate of presidential electors, an independent group had to gather at least 12,000 valid signatures on petitions—which was easy—and to make sure that at least fifty signatures came from each of the state's sixty-two counties —which was sometimes impossible. The same applied to any candidate for state office. At the city level, a candidate for Mayor could be nominated independently by his supporters getting 7,500 valid signatures, with the only restriction being that the signers had not signed primary designating petitions for any other candidate for the same office.

† They lost to La Guardia in 1933, 1937 and 1941; to Impellitteri in 1950 and Lindsay in 1965; winning the mayoralty with O'Brien in 1932, O'Dwyer in 1945 and 1949, and with Wagner in 1953, 1957 and

enrolled Democrats showed they could roll up thundering majorities when they felt like it, and could just as easily vote Republican. The GOP nominees for Senator carried the city twice, and so did a nominee for Judge of the Court of Appeals. On other occasions, Democratic candidates for Governor and President did so poorly with their own folk that they needed the vote of splinter parties to outpoll the Republicans.*

What it added up to was this:

New York City thought of itself as a Democratic stronghold; its voters actually preferred to vote Democratic and did so routinely for offices and candidates who did not figure in the headlines. But if an attractive independent hat was tossed into the ring, or somebody shouted "down with the bosses," the voters were apt to throw party ties to the wind and vote as they damn well pleased for the moment. About the only thing they ever drew the line at was electing as Mayor any Republican foolhardy enough to run as such.

The formally organized legal † parties which figured importantly in elections were:

---

1961. For other city offices in special elections, Taylor won for Controller in 1934 by only 16,000 votes; Brunner won for President of the Board of Aldermen in the 1936 landslide year, and Sharkey was defeated by Rudolph Halley for President of the successor City Council in 1951.

* Irving M. Ives and Jacob Javits carried New York City on the Republican ticket for Senator in 1952 and 1962. Kenneth Keating was the Court of Appeals candidate in 1965 who did the same thing. James M. Mead in 1946, Walter A. Lynch in 1950, and Adlai Stevenson in 1956 carried the city only with minor party votes.

† A legal party under the election law was one that had polled at least 50,000 votes for Governor—no other office would do—at the preceding gubernatorial election. A party legal at the state level was also legal for city elections. It was entitled, as long as it retained its standing, to enroll its voters at registration time, and hold primary elections, at public expense, for the selection of its nominees for both public and party offices.

TABULATION OF VOTE CAST IN NEW YORK CITY UNDER THE PRINCIPAL PARTY EMBLEMS
FOR THE CANDIDATES FOR THE MAJOR OFFICE AT STAKE IN THE YEARS LISTED

| Year | Office | Dem. | Rep. | Soc. | Comm. | Fusion | Recovery |
|---|---|---|---|---|---|---|---|
| 1932 | President | Roosevelt 1,455,176 | Hoover 584,056 | Thomas 122,565 | Foster 24,212 | | |
| 1933 | Mayor | O'Brien 586,672 | La Guardia 446,833 | Solomon 59,846 | Minor 26,044 | La Guardia 421,689 | McKee 609,053 |
| 1934 | Governor | Lehman 1,210,515 | Moses 406,558 | Solomon 77,615 | Amter 41,229 | | **American Labor** |
| 1936 | President | Roosevelt 1,802,502 | Landon 665,951 | Thomas 38,520 | Browder 31,952 | | Roosevelt 238,845 |
| 1937 | Mayor | Mahoney 890,756 | La Guardia 674,611 | | | La Guardia 187,229 | La Guardia 482,796 |
| 1938 | Governor | Lehman 1,127,261 | Dewey 785,641 | Thomas 17,406 | | | Lehman 349,749 |
| 1940 | President | Roosevelt 1,649,074 | Willkie 1,247,074 | Thomas 12,394 | | | Roosevelt 317,009 |
| 1941 | Mayor | O'Dwyer 1,054,235 | La Guardia 668,485 | Hartmann 22,616 | | La Guardia 82,659 | La Guardia 435,374 |
| 1942 | Governor | Bennett 822,916 | Dewey 737,652 | Cheney 17,622 | Amter 42,040 | **Liberal** | Alfange 346,557 |
| 1944 | President | Roosevelt 1,151,678 | Dewey 1,274,128 | Thomas 5,521 | | Roosevelt 306,642 | Roosevelt 389,999 |

# The Parties

| Year | Office | | | No-Deal Party | | |
|------|--------|---|---|---|---|---|
| 1945 | Mayor | O'Dwyer 867,426 | Goldstein 310,448 | Morris 408,408 | Goldstein 122,316 | O'Dwyer 257,929 |
| 1946 | Governor | Mead 850,504 | Dewey 1,182,270 | | Mead 163,325 | Mead 453,426 |
| 1948 | President | Truman 1,403,379 | Dewey 1,108,218 | | Truman 193,166 | Wallace 422,355 |
| 1949 | Mayor | O'Dwyer 1,266,512 | Morris 570,713 | | Morris 373,287 | Marcantonio 356,626 |
| 1950 | Governor | Lynch 1,033,198 | Dewey 1,119,450 | | Lynch 241,831 | McManus 176,202 |
| 1952 | President | Stevenson 1,517,982 | Eisenhower 1,495,491 | | Stevenson 336,948 | Halliman 56,647 |
| 1953 | Mayor | Wagner 1,022,626 | Riegelman 661,591 | | Halley 428,688 | McAvoy 53,045 |
| 1954 | Governor | Harriman 1,260,426 | Ives 765,464 | | Harriman 203,693 | McManus 39,738 |
| 1956 | President | Stevenson 1,383,092 | Eisenhower 1,553,298 | | Stevenson 231,784 | |
| 1957 | Mayor | Wagner 1,291,724 | Christenberry 585,738 | | Wagner 217,941 | |
| 1958 | Governor | Harriman 1,116,814 | Rockefeller 1,011,814 | | Harriman 205,221 | |

TABULATION OF VOTE CAST IN NEW YORK CITY UNDER THE PRINCIPAL PARTY EMBLEMS
FOR THE CANDIDATES FOR THE MAJOR OFFICE AT STAKE IN THE YEARS LISTED

| Year | Office | Dem. | Rep. | Civil Service | Liberal | Citizens Party | Conservative |
|------|--------|------|------|---------------|---------|----------------|--------------|
| 1960 | President | Kennedy 1,646,214 | Nixon 1,145,205 | | Kennedy 290,109 | | |
| 1961 | Mayor | Wagner 1,026,246 | Lefkowitz 835,691 | | Wagner 211,175 | Gerosa 321,604 | |
| 1962 | Governor | Morgenthau 1,118,215 | Rockefeller 1,078,293 | | Morgenthau 161,697 | | Jaquith 50,184 |
| 1964 | President | Johnson 2,009,433 | Goldwater 801,877 | | Johnson 174,210 | | |
| 1965 | Mayor | Beame 983,109 | Lindsay 867,310 | Beame 63,590 | Lindsay 281,796 | | Buckley 341,226 |

# The Parties

VOTER ENROLLMENT IN THE PARTIES LEGALLY CONSTITUTED
AS SUCH UNDER THE ELECTION LAW IN THE YEARS LISTED

| Year | Dem. | Rep. | Soc. | Comm. | | Blank |
|---|---|---|---|---|---|---|
| 1932 | 1,652,140 | 449,166 | 34,835 | | | 200,036 |
| 1933 | 1,643,784 | 435,966 | 26,303 | 8,952 | | 192,761 |
| 1934 | 1,490,213 | 320,075 | 19,299 | 9,902 | | 135,822 |
| 1936 | 2,289,213 | 413,527 | 12,564 | 10,463 | | 174,417 |
| | | | | | **ALP** | |
| 1937 | 1,756,288 | 367,360 | 8,271 | | 205,358 | 145,988 |
| 1938 | 1,676,203 | 398,700 | 7,524 | | 205,789 | 145,760 |
| 1940 | 2,273,367 | 758,385 | | | 150,763 | 207,945 |
| 1941 | 1,720,024 | 407,020 | | | 175,637 | 149,413 |
| 1942 | 1,415,341 | 401,511 | | | 180,442 | 125,875 |
| 1944 | 1,978,101 | 821,013 | | | 194,602 | 223,475 |
| 1945 | 1,436,928 | 349,132 | | | 223,232 | 168,411 |
| 1946 | 1,555,661 | 714,946 | | | 252,313 | 190,183 |
| | | | **Liberal** | | | |
| 1948 | 1,939,393 | 842,824 | 93,250 | | 199,947 | 238,836 |
| 1949 | 1,818,812 | 484,722 | 112,859 | | 164,229 | 194,702 |
| 1950 | 1,825,247 | 566,072 | 107,850 | | 98,173 | 209,551 |
| 1952 | 2,132,181 | 962,599 | 90,229 | | 52,734 | 252,750 |
| 1953 | 1,606,275 | 506,931 | 92,655 | | 32,937 | 158,060 |
| 1954 | 1,708,597 | 516,075 | 58,862 | | 21,185 | 160,736 |
| 1956 | 2,087,495 | 923,062 | 67,132 | | | 169,246 |
| 1957* | 1,677,308 | 548,556 | 55,865 | | | 123,628 |
| 1958 | 1,832,921 | 607,415 | 61,617 | | | 136,921 |
| 1960 | 2,376,476 | 841,105 | 73,719 | | | 178,473 |
| 1961 | 2,202,161 | 767,526 | 67,541 | | | 164,518 |
| 1962 | 2,193,159 | 757,985 | 65,629 | | | 164,181 |
| | | | | | **Conservative** | |
| 1964 | 2,377,891 | 697,594 | 62,794 | 8,686 | | 174,577 |

* Permanent personal registration went into effect with the 1957 election. Since people formerly enrolled each year as they registered, the enrollment fluctuated more with their attitude toward the election ahead. Since 1957, it has stabilized, though the voting tendencies have not.

# The Parties

The Republicans and the Democrats, who always met the legal requirements they had collaborated in establishing.

The Socialist party, once an important force because of its appeal to the foreign-born. Unable to compete ideologically with the leftward push of the Democrats in the days of the New Deal, it lost official status in 1938.

The Communist party, good for at least 100,000 votes in a state election prior to the Cold War, deliberately gave up official standing at the 1936 election so that its members could enroll in and thus infiltrate the new American Labor Party then being formed.

The American Labor party, which was started as a labor arm of the New Deal in 1936, established itself as an official party at that same election, and figured thereafter as a steadfast supporter of La Guardia in mayoralty elections. The Communist infiltration of 1936 became domination by 1944 and when even the Communists had exhausted the propaganda value of the ALP name, it passed out of existence at the 1954 election.

The Liberal party, formed for the 1944 Presidential election by most of the labor leaders who had originated the ALP, left it because they wouldn't live under the same political roof as the Communists.

The Conservative party, formed by right-wing Republicans in 1962 because they saw Governor Nelson Rockefeller as too leftish, achieved full party status that same year and continued to show strength in the 1965 mayoralty election and the 1966 gubernatorial election.

Independent groups were numerous at the city level, simply because they were easy to set up and maintain. Once one got the necessary petitions, and registered the name, its leadership could make its decisions in a hotel room, or even a telephone booth. It never held a primary election, or enrolled its voters, so that there never was a count of noses.

The rub, if any, came in the securing of independent nominating petitions, but here, too, the operating rules were in their favor. Both primary designating petitions for legal parties, and independent petitions for groups had to be filed with the Board of Elections, which was notorious for tossing out petitions for flimsy reasons. There was the timeworn story of how the Board, faced with an absolutely perfect bulletproof set of primary petitions filed by an insurgent, rejected them anyhow. It held that no one could possibly prepare legitimate petitions that were so error free, and that the ones before the Board were therefore fraudulent on their face.

But the Board, always manned by party regulars, and concerned with keeping the status quo within each party, never was so hard on independent petitions which didn't touch the major party hierarchies. There was no recallable instance of an independent office seeker, with a broad base of support, having been kept off the ballot by technicalities conjured up for the moment. Also, the civil courts, to which Board of Elections rulings could be appealed, were more lenient for independents, even when they seemed to lack popular backing.

It should be made clear that there was nothing necessarily holy about independent candidacies. The major ones reflected splits within either the Democratic or Republican ranks which were not, or could not be settled in a regular primary election.*

A second category included those designed to attract inde-

---

* The independent mayoralty candidacy of Joseph V. McKee on the Recovery party ticket in 1933 stemmed from the hope of Bronx

pendent support for major party figures who would also be running under other labels that might be less palatable, such as the City Fusion party nominations of La Guardia, running also as a Republican, in 1933 and 1937; also the Brotherhood party set up by Democratic labor unions in 1961 to back Bob Wagner for Mayor in case he lost out in the Democratic primary, and had only the Liberal party line to offer.

Then there were also the labels without significance—just manufactured by major party nominees to snag a vote here and there, such as Louis Lefkowitz' Civic Action and Non-Partisan additions to his Republican line for Mayor in 1961, or Bob Wagner's City Fusion line in 1957, after that group had long been only a shell of a shell.

Finally, there were the perennials of the left, the Socialist Labor, Workers and Industrial Government groups, which somehow always got on the ballot and rarely polled votes equal to the signatures they had obtained.

On the face of a New York City voting machine the first column always went to the party which had polled the largest vote for Governor. The Republicans held this honor after the 1938 election, when the Democratic majority was obtained with the help of the ALP, and the Democrats never regained first place, by themselves, in the years thereafter.

What follows is a close look at the parties themselves.

---

boss Edward J. Flynn that it would help salvage his local ticket in the Bronx from otherwise certain defeat; the candidacy of Newbold Morris, Republican, on the No Deal party for Mayor in 1945 was inspired by an ailing La Guardia to make sure that the Republican-Liberal coalition which had rejected further sponsorship of La Guardia would be unable to win with anyone else; the candidacy of Vincent Impellitteri for Mayor in 1950 came after Impy had been turned down by Tammany; and that of Lawrence Gerosa, Bronx Democrat, on the Citizens' party for Mayor in 1961 was a warm-up for the Conservative party's emergence, statewide, the following year.

# The Parties

## THE GOP

The Republican party was assigned the loser's role in city politics four years before the city was formed, and it has played the part conscientiously ever since. In any other business but politics, it would have folded, or changed its name, or gone into another line. But the state and national Republican parties needed a local branch, for election law purposes if nothing else.

The appointment as perpetual underdog was not one the local Republicans sought at the start or relished in the later decades. It was handed to them, willy-nilly, by the upstate Republicans, in this fashion:

In 1894, when the consolidation of New York City was in the offing, there was also a state constitutional convention that the GOP controlled. With full knowledge of what they were doing, the upstaters wrote into the new basic law provisions that made certain the New York City-to-be never would be entitled to a majority in either house of the Legislature, no matter how big the city grew.*

In thus protecting upstate against the city, the rural bloc gave the New York City Republicans the job of running an anti-city party within the city, hardly a local vote-getting formula. In the first place, the idea that acres counted more

---

* The day the provision was adopted by the convention, Charles Z. Lincoln, a leading delegate, remarked to his fourteen-year-old son, "I believe we made sure today that in my lifetime, and probably yours as well, the city will never control the Legislature." The conversation was recounted to the author by the son, Leroy A. Lincoln, before his death in 1957. In 1910, 1912, 1934 and 1964, statewide election disasters for the GOP resulted in enough upstate Democrats being elected to turn control of both houses over to the Democratic party, though the city's ration of members remained constant.

53

than people did not sit well with the city's immigrant population, which remembered firsthand the superior rights of the landholder over the peasant in the old country.

Secondly, and more lastingly, it turned the almost invariably Republican-controlled Legislature into the bulwark of the railroads, the streetcar magnates, the gas and electric companies, the factory and real estate owners, against the constituent-conscious crowd from New York who howled for low trolley and subway fares, eighty-cent gas, cheap electricity, workmen's compensation, minimum wage and maximum hour laws, factory and tenement house inspection.

In the early years the "interests" bought some legislators of either party with equal aplomb, but overall the picture was that of the Democrats standing up and yelling for the rights of the people, while the top GOP hierarchy preached the sanctity of private property and quoted the Constitution and the Founding Fathers by rote on any social issue.

The original GOP position was an albatross even in recent times, and after repeated lickings, manifested by a dragging of the feet on popular issues in New York like rent control. Even as of 1965, the people's distrust of the Republicans when involved in local issues was so obvious that when John V. Lindsay announced his candidacy for Mayor, his opening remarks were that he was running as "John Lindsay, not as a Republican."

The voters, scared by the Republicans and spoon-fed by the Democrats on local issues, did not react consistently against the GOP in state and national elections. The ranks, so sparse on local issues, were fortified in national elections by the phenomenon known as the "fourth year Republican," who appeared at the polls only to vote for President, then went into political hibernation for another four years.

## The Parties

Even earlier there was the small businessman who voted Democratic for local office, even for Governor if Alfred E. Smith was running, but who voted Republican for President on the theory that the Republican Party was good for business. He was joined in this by many a laboring man who accepted the "full dinner pail" slogan of William McKinley. There were enough of these at various times to give William Howard Taft a city majority over William Jennings Bryan, for Warren G. Harding and then Calvin Coolidge to sweep all five boroughs, and even to hold down Al Smith's margin on his own sidewalks to permit Herbert Hoover to carry the state. But all of this was pre-1929, pre-depression, pre-New Deal.

A reaction against the Democratic swing to the left has manifested itself every four years in Queens and Richmond. Every Republican nominee for President, starting with the election of 1940 and continuing through 1956, carried Queens, which would vote Democratic in between. Little Richmond even went for Richard Nixon in the 1960 election. It represented, in essence, middle-class reaction, rather than affirmative Republican strength, showing itself in state elections as well.

But none of these ever helped the Republicans maintain an effective party organization locally, or even to control their own destinies. Doomed to dependence on the turn of a wheel that might put a Republican in the White House, or in the Executive Mansion in Albany, the local Republicans learned also to look outside the city for policy and leadership.

For decades when the Republican Old Guard ran the party in the nation and the state, the local GOP took its orders from the National Committeeman, Charles D. Hilles, courtly and charming representative of big business. The next real leader

55

was Tom Dewey, whose influence began in 1938 with his first race for Governor, and lasted through 1960, who will be treated in Chapter 4 on the Bosses.

In the course of events, the local Republicans saw good times as well as bad. If the party was entrenched in Washington, it fared quite well on a diet of federal judges, United States marshals and commissioners, federal attorneys and their staffs, and receivers in bankruptcy. In the days of Prohibition, a Republican so minded could even grow rich on the federal end of the dry law evasion—withdrawal permits of alcohol theoretically distilled for medicinal purposes. Years later, with the Republicans in control at Albany, another variation in the liquor trade made some party bigwigs prosperous, and got them in trouble over the granting of liquor licenses for cash.

In poor times, the county organizations learned to rely on handouts from their friendly Democratic counterparts in return for not creating unnecessary trouble at the polls. In the Bronx the man who was Republican County Chairman for twenty years held a public sinecure by appointment of the Democratic judges, at the behest of the Democratic boss. His district leaders were equally assured protection against starvation. It was a solution easy for the Republicans to rationalize. It made no sense to them to fight the Democrats tooth and nail, on the wrong side of all the issues, and lose by a margin of 3 to 1, when by relaxing and losing by 4 to 1, their opponents would help keep some kind of an organization alive.

In Manhattan and Brooklyn, the Republicans usually put up a fight whenever it was worthwhile—which was seldom—but also had loose and less obvious arrangements with the Democrats. If new judgeships were allocated to the county, they were divided between the parties, with the Democrats getting the lion's share. This was usually assured by a hand-shake agreement before the Legislature enacted the measure creating the jobs. The Republican control of the Legislature gave the local Republicans other controls as well. Legislation important to a county Democratic organization might be enacted only if the GOP in the same county was cut in, or guaranteed a deal in a different area.

In Queens and Richmond, where the Republicans were in the majority, on and off, as a result of national swings, the local Republicans fought or traded as the situation warranted.

By the use of the gerrymander in laying out the legislative seats allowed the city, the Republicans were able to maintain districts here and there that could be counted safe for their Congressional, State Senate or Assembly nominees.

With the city, state and nation committed by court edict to the rule of one person, one vote, the underrepresentation in the Legislature that automatically cast the Republicans as the anti-city party disappeared as a factor. It remained for the reorientation of the Republican party nationally to determine the policies that would change the political life of the big-city voter one way or another.

## The Democratic Machines

In the years of their greatest power and glory—the quarter century from 1910 to 1935—the Democratic party machines could count on at least 30,000 eager commandos, willing to hustle votes for any Democratic ticket at each and every election. These cadres were the county committeemen provided for in the election law, which allowed each party in each county to determine how many committeemen it wanted. The Democrats, particularly in Tammany Hall, took full advantage of the provision; they had the manpower others did not.

In theory, this gave the Democrats a broader base than any other party to which they could point with pride as representing the ultimate in democracy. The enrolled voters in each area, sometimes no larger than one heavily populated city block, would elect four of five county committeemen whose names were on the primary election ballot. One of those so elected would be tabbed the election district captain. He and the captains from other districts would meet in the local clubhouse and elect the district leader. He in turn would meet with his peers at county headquarters and elect the county boss.

In practice the county committees were too large to do anything much but meet once and delegate their power to the next layer above them in the hierarchy. As a result, the man at the top of the pyramid, the county boss, could wield his power, once obtained, to influence the picking of the district leader by the giving or withholding of job patronage to the district. The district leader in turn, rather than being the creature of the district captains, had picked them himself when he made up the county committee slate for the voters to pass on.

The power ran both uphill and down, based as it was on reciprocity—you scratch my back and I'll scratch yours. The district captain knew every voter in his district—or else. Anyone with troubles—an eviction notice from the landlord, a family member arrested after a brawl, a summons to jury duty or a traffic ticket, the need for a small loan or a permanent job —saw the district captain first. The captain took the problem to the district leader, with a verbal report on how many votes there were in the family, and whether the party owed them a favor for past support, or could hope for their votes henceforth.

If something could be done, the district leader spoke the appropriate word in the appropriate place, to the judge, the court clerk, or the police captain in the local precinct. If the family needed cash and groceries, the district leader supplied a few bucks himself, sent word to the corner grocer to restore credit, or sent the family breadwinner to the local public utility for a job digging ditches in the streets.

Come election time, the district captain made the rounds, again and again, not overlooking the possibility of a single vote, reminding of past favors, promising future ones, doing anything to get the voters to the polls in a state of mind friendly to the Democratic ticket. If he produced the votes he was rewarded with a city job, or promoted in the one he had. Many a seemingly senseless election fraud stemmed from nothing more than an ambitious captain trying to make his district, and hence himself, look better in the eyes of the district leader. The district leader, in turn, claiming patronage for his district, did so on the basis of the majority *he* had turned in.

By dint of 30,000 workers, the Democratic party could count on a minimum of 700,000 hard-core voters, who felt they owed the party something, or looked forward to the day when they would. This was a comfortable number to have stowed away, especially when the total vote was well under 2,000,000.

It gave the party bosses the right—which they exercised—to tell the men they had nominated and elected, particularly men with no substantial following outside the party, of the jobs and favor patronage expected, patronage needed by them for continuing power, or cash.

# The Parties

Those days have disappeared. Every battalion of commandos came down to the size of a squad. The incentive to devote long hours to vote-hustling was no longer there for the professionals. The Democratic party machinery did not control a substantial segment of the vote. Ironically, the hardest blows at the old system were struck by two men for whom the party had rolled up record majorities—Franklin D. Roosevelt for Governor and President, Robert F. Wagner, Jr., for Mayor.

The collapse of the political machines all over the country as a result of the social reforms of the New Deal was first noted by this author in a *Saturday Evening Post* article in 1947 entitled "Political Machines Have Lost Their Grip." Were it to be written today, it would be amended to read "Have Lost Their All." Welfare, unemployment insurance, social security and union pensions cut down on the district captain's monopoly as the helper of the family in distress. Roosevelt's dicta that a man in public office owed the public an explanation of how he made a fortune took away the incentive of the abler district leaders to stay in politics, since they no longer dared hold sinecure public posts while grafting. The business of being ethical turned out to be contagious. The courts got fussy about fixing jury notices and in 1950 the fix-proof traffic ticket was invented, though for a while the public didn't realize it. District leaders paid the fines out of their own pockets rather than admit their helplessness.

Wagner, who came in as Mayor knowing the machine operation as well as anyone, gave the city employees—who even under Civil Service included the very best district captains—collective bargaining and career and salary plans that destroyed at one fell swoop the obligation of the employees to the party or the administration in power. From then on, they could get their pay raises and benefits automatically, or by collective bargaining, without wearing themselves out as party workers in their spare time. The old promotion and merit raise system within Civil Service stopped functioning for the district captain.

Wagner, courting labor and social welfare groups rather than the party machines, was able to build up his own informal organization and it was good enough to beat the regular organization in his fight in the 1961 primary. There had been two previous great primary fights for Mayor—Walker versus Hylan in 1925 and Wagner versus Impellitteri in 1953, but in each of these, the winner had the support of the organization in two counties, New York and The Bronx. In 1961 Wagner defeated all five county organizations combined.

The organization, by then, could no longer even control a primary because it lacked interested district captains to canvass the vote—with no reward in sight for so doing, and the obligation of the voter to the district captain became nonexistent. The captain no longer knew the voters, and the voters didn't know him.

Finally, there developed the Reform Democrats. They started in a small way, in the wealthy Park Avenue section of Manhattan. Young men home from World War II, with interests broader than the jobs to which they had returned, directed themselves to politics and civic affairs. So did their wives. Most of them were well enough off to be independent of the financial rewards of politics. On the issues of reform and greater democracy, they won control of the party organization in the "silk-stocking" area.

The movement was spread by the candidacy of Adlai Stevenson for President. His intellectual appeal, while it won him no elections, drew thousands of young men and women to participate in Democratic Party politics. When they found the old-line district clubs not particularly hospitable, they formed their own rival clubs, and sought control in the primaries.

There were major differences between the new clubs and the old. The old were brought up on the maxims of "my party, right or wrong," and "I stick with my leader." The new groups were dedicated to the theory that government was too important to leave to the politicians, that the end justified the means, and that their party had damn well better be right, or they wouldn't support it. Their slogan was "down with the bosses."

The Democratic state convention of 1958 brought things to a boil. Carmine De Sapio, then boss of Tammany, looking ahead to the national convention of 1960, which he thought might produce a winner, had formed a statewide coalition to control the national convention delegates-to-be. A first demonstration of strength, two years in advance, was to unite behind the ultra-respectable District Attorney Frank S. Hogan of New York as the nominee for United States Senator. The reformers, with the support of Mrs. Eleanor Roosevelt and former Governor Herbert H. Lehman, backed Thomas K. Finletter, a Stevenson associate. Governor Averell Harriman, who should have been in control since he too was up for election, tried to ride two horses, saying he would happily run with either Finletter or Thomas E. Murray, Jr., of the Atomic Energy Commission, who was privately Harriman's first choice.

In an open roll call, Hogan easily defeated the divided opposition, but that settled nothing. De Sapio, as an appeasement move, put the reformers in charge of a coordinating committee to run the Harriman-Hogan campaign. Never was a campaign run with more appearances of sabotage from within. During and after the campaign, the reformers attacked the convention and inferentially the ticket, as "boss-ridden." Harriman, due to lose anyhow to the then fresh and attractive Nelson Rockefeller, was slaughtered; the first incumbent Governor to be defeated in a reelection bid since Nathan L. Miller, Republican, in 1922. Hogan, running against a then totally unknown Kenneth Keating, should have won but lost.

The loss of City Hall to John V. Lindsay on the Republican-Liberal ticket in 1965 caused no tears among the Reformers. Many of them sat on their hands during the campaign, like West Side Congressman William Fitts Ryan, who never sent a sound truck through the streets of his Democratic area for the head of the Democratic ticket, from the beginning of the campaign to the end. Others, like the people who had just defeated De Sapio for district leader for the third time in Greenwich Village, came out openly for Lindsay's election, even though they had participated earlier in the Democratic primary election.

To the professional in politics, a man who attends a party convention and casts his vote on the losing side, or who runs a slate and votes in a primary, has lost his right to bolt. To them, it is a case of majority rule, and anyone who doesn't want to abide by that shouldn't go to the convention, or run in the primary, but should operate outside the party controls.

With the old Democratic organizations losing prestige, and the political independents on the rise, problems as to the future of the Democratic Party in the city and state were apparent in 1966.

# The Parties

## THE LIBERAL PARTY

To understand the Liberal party—which is sort of a cross between a state of mind and an Elks Convention—one turns back to 1936. As Franklin D. Roosevelt prepared to run for a second term, the leaders of the garment industry unions in New York City cast aside as out-dated Samuel Gompers' perennial admonition that labor unions should reward their friends, punish their enemies, but stay away from political affiliation. The New Yorkers formed, under the name of the American Labor party, a political organization designed to be the labor arm of the Roosevelt New Deal in New York State.

Roosevelt himself encouraged, even privately sponsored the move. Although Ed Flynn and National Chairman James A. Farley warned him that the Democrats might rue the day, the President laughed and told them to give the union people whatever help they needed. Flynn and Farley obeyed.

The union leaders who emerged overnight as politicians were David Dubinsky, Sidney Hillman, Jacob Potofsky and Luigi Antonini, all from the garment industry, with their principal agent and deputy a millinery union leader named Alex Rose. The party changed its name, en route, but in 1966 Rose was still running the show, with Dubinsky and Potofsky in the background, while Hillman and Antonini were dead.

As noted earlier, the Communists infiltrated the original ALP from the word "go," even though they and the garment union leaders were deadly enemies. The hatred stemmed from the fact that during the late 1920's, Dubinsky's and Hillman's unions had hired gangsters to run the Reds out of the garment trades, the Commies fought back with other thugs and there were gang killings on both sides.

# The Parties

It took the Communists about six years to gain control of the ALP county organizations in Manhattan, Brooklyn and Queens, with control of the state committee in the offering. In 1944, Hillman had reached national position as Roosevelt's go-between with organized labor. To keep a united front for the fourth-term campaign, Hillman made a deal with the Communists. Its terms were that he and his union, one of the two largest in the garment trades, would stay within the ALP without fighting the Communists any further, if, they in turn agreed never to nominate any identified Communists for public office as ALP candidates.

Dubinsky, a long-standing rival of Hillman in the trade union field, led Rose, Potofsky and others out of the ALP, along with the unions they controlled, and formed the Liberal party. They stayed with it through the years in which it took over the original role designed for the ALP, while the latter withered and died.

At the start the union leaders and their memberships had no great interest in patronage or public jobholding. Their concern was the continuation and broadening of social reforms through political action. The party workers were men who were organizers and shop stewards in the constituent unions, just doubling in brass as political workers. Ideology was more important than a power structure.

In theory they never abandoned this concept. In practice the party, time and time again, was able to find virtue in a combination of convenience and necessity which brings it down more to the plane of the major parties.

Note, for instance:

In 1950, O'Dwyer's resignation forced a special election for the mayoralty job he vacated at the same time that a Governor and United States Senator were to be chosen. Rose made a

deal with Flynn of The Bronx and De Sapio of Tammany
that if the Democrats would nominate Democratic Supreme
Court Justice Ferdinand Pecora—Dubinsky's favorite gin
rummy opponent for Mayor—the Liberals would also nominate him. Both parties would rally behind Herbert H. Lehman
for his first full term in the Senate, and the Liberals would
nominate for Governor any one of three the Democrats
picked: Court of Appeals Judge Albert Conway, a conservative; Court of Appeals Judge Charles S. Desmond, a middle-
of-the-roader; or Representative Walter A. Lynch of The
Bronx, who had a liberal record in Congress. The emphasis
on ideology seemed slight.

The Liberal party nomination of Franklin D. Roosevelt,
Jr., for Governor in 1966 was based less on approval of the
son of the late President than it was on two other factors,
neither ideological in base. The first was that the leaders hoped
—it turned out to be in vain—that the Roosevelt name
would enable the party to outpoll the new rival Conservative
party; the second was that the leadership, not consulted on
the identity of the Democratic standard-bearer, wanted to
show the Democrats how much they needed the Liberal
party support.

One difference still remained between the Liberal party and
the two major parties. Control of Liberal party affairs by the
top hierarchy had never been contested in a primary. Its decisions on whom to endorse among major party nominees are
incontestable because of a law passed in the late 1940's aimed
at keeping the ALP's Vito Marcantonio out of the Republican
and Democratic primaries. The Wilson-Pakula Law limited
contestants in a party primary to persons enrolled in that
party, unless given special permission to enter by the appropriate party committee. Abe Beame's request for permission

to enter the Liberal party primary, to give the rank and file Liberals a right to choose between him and Lindsay, was a campaign gesture that Beame was certain would be turned down. It was.

## THE CONSERVATIVE PARTY

This group came into being as an offshoot of the Republican party just as the Liberal party grew from Democratic stock. Its goal was to lead the Republican policies in the state and nation to the political right, the way the Liberals were supposed to keep the Democrats to the political left. While the Democratic-Liberal alliance was frequently successful, practical obstacles to similar Conservative success arose from the very start.

The Conservatives achieved party status with their first candidate for Governor, David H. Jaquith, in 1962. Rolling up 141,877 votes for Jaquith, relatively unknown, on their first try was a substantial achievement. But as far as influencing Republican policies or the election result, the operation was a total loss. Nelson Rockefeller, running for reelection as a "liberal" Republican, amassed a statewide margin of 529,000 over his Democratic opponent, despite the Jaquith vote. The identical thing happened in 1966, though this time the Conservatives rose to third place by outpolling the Liberals.

In 1964 the Republican national ticket represented the Conservative dream. However, the party as such could not put up a slate of electors under its own emblem, pledged to Barry Goldwater and William Miller. Unless the Conservative slate was identical with the Republican slate of electors, the votes for the two could not be lumped in the counting. The Republicans refused to let their electors run also as Conservatives. Assumedly, the Conservatives voted under the Republican emblem, but an all-time low number of Republicans followed suit. The ticket fell to an impossible nadir, failing to carry a single county of the sixty-two in the state, though there were several dozen that had never voted Democratic since the two-party system began.

The combination of the Rockefeller win and the Goldwater debacle was hardly an object lesson for the Republican state leaders of any local advantages in the Goldwater approach, and therefore no reason at all for welcoming a Conservative party alliance based on ideological concessions.

However, the 1965 mayoralty election demonstrated a definite appeal of the Conservative philosophy to some voters in the Democratic ranks, chiefly in Queens and Richmond and the Bay Ridge section of Brooklyn. These voters had maintained their Democratic enrollment, voted Democratic for Mayor, and voted Republican for President and for Governor for nearly a quarter of a century. They were, in the main, members of the middle class irritated by Democratic national policies that they viewed as fostering a welfare state; who approved of Joseph McCarthy and anyone else who screamed louder about the internal Communist menace; who looked askance at fair housing and civil rights laws; and to whom the final insult was school integration through busing of pupils from one area to another.

In the 1965 mayoralty election, William F. Buckley, the brilliantly cynical Conservative candidate for Mayor, drew more of these votes, previously cast for Democratic mayoralty nominees, than he drew defectors from the Republican column. The result was the election of Lindsay, Buckley's chief target.

However, despite this series of tactical defeats, the proba-

# The Parties

bility existed that those voters already in the Conservative party, drawn from either Republican or Democratic enrollment, would stay with the Conservative party for many years to come, unless either major party switched to the far right, or the John Birch Society absorbed the Republican state and national committees.

# 4. The Bosses

New York was always more than slightly schizoid in its approach to the idea of political bosses. The same citizenry that demanded party unity and responsible political leadership—normally furnished by the boss—would rise in righteous wrath if it got word that someone in a back room was telling elected officials what to do.

The public linked the boss with the memorable Nast cartoon of Tweed, and visualized him as invariably puffing a fat cigar while plotting his own profit and public plunder. What it failed to comprehend was that while the boss did think of private gain, as any other man in business, the successful boss also thought in terms of issues of government. His chief function was to elect his party's candidates, and thus preserve his party's and his own power, and in order to do that he had to court the voter, make sure that his party stayed on top of the issues of the day.

He spent at least as much time in his smoke-filled room working out a party consensus on housing, transportation, social security or race integration as he did on matters of patronage or profit, for without winning elections, there was little patronage and less profit. One of his major tasks, in a city like New York, would be lining up the party's legislators, in the City Council, the state capital or in Washington, for the party program, using both the carrot and the stick to get them to vote as the party image required.

He had to guess right on candidates who not only would owe their nomination to him, but who could be elected after they were nominated. Sometimes he had to sidetrack the man whose loyalty he was sure of in favor of a better vote-getter, making whatever terms he could with the latter, and preferably before the candidate was too sure of election.

The classic example of a political boss giving orders to an elected official involved two leading practitioners; they were Charles F. Murphy, leader of Tammany Hall, and Governor Alfred E. Smith. The time was 1923, and Smith, with Murphy's full support, was looking toward the Democratic nomination for the Presidency, which did not come until five years later. Prohibition was the great political issue of the day.

The New York Legislature had just voted to repeal the Mullan-Gage Law, the state statute that gave local authorities concurrent authority with Federal agents to enforce the Eighteenth Amendment. Smith told Murphy he would veto the repealer, holding it would align him too definitely as a political "wet" to get national convention delegates from the southern and western "dry" states.

Murphy, speaking quietly and solemnly, said:

"Al, if you don't sign the repeal bill, I will never support you again for any office for which you want to run."

Smith signed the measure.

The public never knew of the incident until it began to bob up in memoirs many years later. It would be hard to project what its reaction would have been. But on this occasion, at least, Murphy was thinking in terms of the party as a whole, while Smith was thinking of himself.

The boss system in New York politics was a consistently less spectacular operation than in other cities. The most colorful characters, such as Jimmy Hines, Peter McGuiness, or even Tin Box Tom Farley, were essentially local, though Hines' domain covered half a dozen Manhattan districts. The bosses most completely in control on a broad basis were sometimes not identified as bosses by the public.

There was no big boss as flamboyant as Frank Hague, who ran Hudson County and most of the rest of New Jersey from a plush Manhattan penthouse, and became a millionaire many times over by demanding a percentage of the profits from every contractor building a highway, bridge or overpass, as well as taking a kickback of five percent of the weekly pay of the Jersey City and Hudson County employees whose job security lay in him alone.

His much-quoted boast, "I am the law in Jersey City," was cast up at him by outsiders—not because he proclaimed his power in ordering court clemency for a juvenile offender—but because he used that power to have his police throw union organizers out of town and to protect businessmen with whom he had "arrangements."

New York never had a completely corrupt despot since Tweed, who could hold a candle to Tom Pendergast of Kansas City. Pendergast took graft the way Hague did, but also made a business of protecting the professional criminal and padding the voting rolls with a "stiff" for every legitimate voter. He lost it all playing the horses on such a scale that no Internal Revenue Service could ignore it.

This is not to imply that New York's political bosses were

saints. Some sold judgeships and other public posts for cash. Others made money directly on contracts with the city, or sold the inside track to businessmen doing business with or within the city. There were those who used their positions of party power to fatten their law practices or insurance broker-age. Some combined any and all of the above. And there were also those who spurned graft, or even conflict of interest situations, and used their party posts to increase their feeling of power, or even to promote their own candidates for public office.

After 1930 there were six major political bosses worth appraising. Sketches of them, in alphabetical order, follow:

## John F. Curry

Curry presided over Tammany Hall in the period of its greatest decline as a political force. He did so with the same feeling of resentment against a changing order of things that Winston Churchill had with the end of colonialism, though Curry had neither Churchill's perspective nor his principles.

Curry was the last of the old-time leaders, essentially a patronage politician. As a single district leader, he had been immensely successful. His tiny fief on Manhattan's West Side had accumulated title to more petty patronage than any other in the city. Curry had shown himself head and shoulders above other district leaders in getting jobs for his constituents. The other district leaders admired him for it.

When a vacancy occurred in the leadership of Tammany in the spring of 1929, Curry had backers within the organiza-tion, and Mayor Jimmy Walker preferred Curry to any other possibilities. As Curry took over, and Walker's own election for a second term was certain, the prospects seemed rosy for continuation of the kind of politics Curry knew how to play.

Then, in the space of one year, came the Wall Street crash, the beginning of the long depression, coupled with the Seabury investigation of Tammany corruption. Graft ceased to be amusing or acceptable to a population that was out of work and faced hunger. The shopkeeper who had happily paid small tribute to the police suddenly resented it. The district leader who had fixed a ticket for John Q. Citizen was suddenly less of a hero to Mr. Citizen when he read of the hundreds of thousands of dollars the leader had, but couldn't explain.

The public began to think along two lines that Curry was unable to follow. The first was a raising of the standards of ethics in government and politics; the second was for government action to alleviate hunger and unemployment. Curry was a leader who could look wise without being wise. A man of moderate build, with a delicate white mustache and steel-blue eyes, he would, as he listened, give the appearance of mature and reserved consideration of the issue at stake. But armed as he was with only the folk lore of the district leader, the scope of the impending social revolution remained completely out of his ken.

A perfect example involved the Robin Hood role Tammany had played for many years. A percentage of what it stole was handed out in Christmas and Thanksgiving baskets to the less fortunate in any assembly district. If the leader had prospered more than most, the baskets contained turkeys. When the depression came, neither organized charities or organized politics could meet the demands for food, shelter and employment, though both tried at the beginning. Regular relief for those in need emerged as an obligation of government itself. The first governmental steps in this area were faltering and experimental. One of them involved issuing food tickets entitling the holder to groceries for which the city would later pay the storekeeper.

When John P. O'Brien ran for Mayor in the special election of 1932, as Curry's choice to succeed Walker, the Tammany-controlled Welfare Department gave out food tickets to O'Brien's audiences, but only to those who stayed to the end of the meetings. It never occurred to Curry and his lieutenants that hungry people would resent, rather than appreciate, largesse on those terms, particularly since they were entitled to the food tickets without having to stomach O'Brien's oratory.

Franklin Roosevelt, seeking the presidential nomination in 1932, was willing to accept the support of the delegates Curry and his allies in other counties controlled. Curry, at Walker's directions, threw the strength to Al Smith, even though no love was lost between him and Smith by then. When Roosevelt was nominated, and was almost a sure winner of the election ahead, a smarter boss like Frank Hague switched immediately to the Roosevelt standard. Curry continued the fight, hoping to use control of City Hall and of Albany, if he could get it, to battle the man who would be in the White House.

In September 1932, Curry led a coalition of bosses opposing the nomination of Herbert H. Lehman for Governor, even though Lehman was the choice of Roosevelt and had the active support of Smith. Smith leaned across the conference table in the smoke-filled room and threatened to run for Mayor the following year, and "take the city away from you" unless Curry supported Lehman. Curry sneered, "On what ticket?"

"On a Chinese laundry ticket I can beat you and your crowd," Smith retorted.

As the story was usually told, Curry was supporting John Boyd Thatcher, Mayor of Albany, for the governorship. Actually, Curry was backing Thatcher only in the hope of producing a convention deadlock between the latter and Lehman, which he would then resolve by putting over Samuel Levy, Borough President of Manhattan, as a "compromise." Curry's theory was that much of the backing Lehman had was because, if elected, he would be the state's first Jewish Governor, and he felt that if the nominee was to be a Jew, it should be *his* Jew, Levy. The difference in the public stature of the two men never occurred to him as an obstacle.

By 1934, Curry was a Tammany leader opposed by a Democratic President in Washington, a Democratic Governor in Albany, and Fiorello La Guardia as Mayor. That year his reign came to an end. He had lived by use of the patronage sword and he died politically as it was used against him.

## CARMINE G. DE SAPIO

Six men successfully stumbled into and were tumbled out of the leadership of Tammany Hall in the fifteen years between the end of John F. Curry and the advent of De Sapio. The latter, a tall and handsome fashion plate, was the first Italian to rise to the top in political leadership in the city. He held sway for twelve years—the longest span since Murphy's day—before falling victim to political reforms he instituted and some errors of political judgment.

His background in politics was about as bad as could be conjured up; his record one of the best of any leader of any party in any era. As detailed in Chapter 8, De Sapio was put in as leader by the votes owned by Frank Costello, and he carried out the gangster's mandate to give Tammany a clean, intelligent leadership that would reflect credit on all Italians.

De Sapio from the beginning manifested capacity and breadth of vision, with a quiet reasoned approach to political problems that quickly won the approval of Flynn of The Bronx, top ranking leader in the city and state in that era. Flynn, who had operated unhappily with all of the Tammany bosses since Murphy, told intimates:

"De Sapio is the first I could even sit down and talk with."

The latter discreetly assumed the role of junior partner to Flynn in city affairs, taking full command only after Flynn's death in 1953. In a very brief time he scored phenomenal successes as a picker of winning candidates while bringing Tammany's political thinking generally into the twentieth century.

His approach was twofold. First he canvassed and sought to anticipate the public issues ahead, making sure his party was committed to the popular side. He sought new approaches for a political party in government, constantly advertising Tammany's interest in things other than patronage.

Second, he spent time and thought developing and becoming a political associate of men he regarded as potentials for higher office than those they held. For example, he picked Borough President Robert F. Wagner, Jr. as a prospective Mayor before Wagner had even thought of running. He produced Averell Harriman as a likely Governor, and he made a close friend of Frank S. Hogan, whom he viewed as an alternate for Mayor or the candidate for United States Senator.

In dealing with all three, he played down patronage and

stressed issues; assisting, even prodding them into positions he deemed advantageous on the announced premise that their success was necessary to party success. With immediate winners in Wagner and Harriman, he achieved high stature himself.

It was widely and correctly assumed that De Sapio made money during his years as leader that he would not have made had he not been the city and state political boss. It was equally true that no man he backed and elected could ever complain that he had his skirts smeared by scandal emanating from De Sapio's activities.

On one widely publicized occasion, $11,000 in dirty, beaten up but valid currency was found in an envelope in a taxicab that De Sapio had recently vacated. His friend, the professional joke maker Harry Hirschfield, could not resist quipping: "That positively could not be Carmine's money—not that neat clean Carmine with those dirty old bills."

De Sapio's eventual fall from power stemmed from overconfidence approaching vanity, after he himself had opened the door for attacks on the boss structure. Early in the first Wagner administration, De Sapio, seeking to be in the forefront of reform, pushed through rules requiring the direct election of Tammany district leaders by the enrolled voters instead of by the election district captains. It was Tammany's major reform since its emergence as a political rather than a social organization. He told the members of the Tammany executive comittee—the district leaders themselves: "Any leader who can't carry his district with his own name on the ballot hasn't any right to be a leader."

The district leaders, ashamed to plead weakness, reluctantly voted the change.

De Sapio's own home district, at the south end of Greenwich Village, included a large number of his own kinsmen in "Little Italy," and an increasingly large, wealthy and independent population in new apartments on lower Fifth Avenue. He was safely in control of it then, and for years thereafter, and his first error was not quitting as district leader while he was still ahead. He would still have been able to retain leadership of Tammany and his National Committeemanship, plus his unofficial roles as city and state Democratic boss.

By the time he came under the fire of the Reform Movement it was too late for him to quit the district leadership with any grace. It was the only spot in which he was then vulnerable, as a result of population shifts plus the Reform attacks. When he finally was beaten for district leader by the popular voting system he had installed, his whole political pyramid collapsed.

De Sapio's strategy of being out in public, demonstrating the new type of political boss for a new era in politics, made him better known as a person to the public than his predecessors, but in the end the publicity proved a liability rather than an asset.

The Reform Movement showed its muscle when it defeated an incumbent Congressman in a primary fight waged up and down Manhattan's West Side. The Reformers pasted a label "De Sapio's candidate" across the bottom of the campaign posters of their congressional target. The public knew De Sapio's name. When it was used as an epithet of the labels and blared forth as such from the sound trucks, it sank in. "De Sapio" became a bad word without any new political revelations to justify it.

The success of the technique impressed Mayor Wagner. Originally De Sapio's protégé, he came to the conclusion that if he ran for a third term, he would be defeated by the Reformers using the same approach on a broader scale. He also had leaned politically on Herbert H. Lehman and Eleanor Roosevelt, spearheading the reform drive on a city-wide basis. So the Mayor, with a delicate sense for self-protection, cast aside the political leader he had hailed publicly and privately as the best he had ever known. The Mayor joined with the reform band in the hue and cry for De Sapio's head, but since he never trusted their affection for him, he gave them De Sapio's ouster, but not control of the party.

De Sapio never forgave the Mayor. On the other hand, the Mayor in subsequent troubled situations involving the Reformers, was heard sighing and voicing the wish that Reform had never happened and De Sapio was still boss.

## THOMAS E. DEWEY

Tom Dewey was so much a success as racket-buster and vote-getter that the public never realized he was not a political reformer. He played the game as a pragmatist, with the end always justifying the means. For nearly a quarter of a century he was the cold, efficient behind-the-scenes boss of the Republican party in the city and the state. He directed the election of legislative leaders, passed on nominees for the judiciary, selected statewide tickets, made or unmade state and county chairmen of his party. His domination of his party was more complete than Charles F. Murphy's had ever been in Tammany Hall.

The rules were very simple. If a Republican opposed Dewey he was through, politically. If he went along with Dewey, he was safe. If he went along with Dewey, and had the ability to serve him well in political or governmental operations, his future was rosy and security was guaranteed.

It was small wonder that few Republicans liked him, and even fewer opposed him. But to the party as a whole, he was the first meal ticket in decades, and they would have accepted his leadership if he had had two large heads instead of only one.

He showed his vote-getting strength quite early. When he was elected District Attorney of New York County in 1937, as a climax to two years of racket-busting as special prosecutor, he was so well-known that people in other counties looked for his name on their ballots, too. When he ran for Governor in 1938, he came very close to defeating Herbert H. Lehman's fourth-term campaign, even though Lehman was one of the best Governors the state had ever had.

These demonstrations of strength gave him his base for political power. The Republican leadership was furnished at that time by a group of county chairmen of the dozen principal counties of the state. Most of them immediately adopted Dewey as their boy, their first potential winner, and he pledged them his loyalty when he assumed major office, which all assumed would be shortly. The few who balked and stayed off the bandwagon rapidly lost out. Once the mutual assistance pact went into effect, there was scant opportunity to renege.

John R. Crews, the Kings County leader, remarked at a public dinner: "The funny thing about this guy Dewey is that every time he runs for President, he gets elected Governor."

Crews' mot had more behind it than met the ear. Dewey had established himself as a politician who kept his word, who would reward his friends, at any cost, and punish his enemies at any cost, as long as he had the power to do so. The power stemmed from holding the governorship and seeking the presidency. If he obtained the latter it meant a real pot of gold. And if he didn't make the presidency, he was still Governor. No one made any bones about this, not even Dewey. At a caucus of Republican national convention delegates in Chicago in 1952, as Dewey cracked the whip for Eisenhower, he told the Taft supporters in the New York delegation:

"Don't forget I'm still going to be Governor."

This public threat, and many private ones conveyed to the delegates by emissaries, cut the Taft strength of 17 out of 100 down to one out of 100. It represented a switch of 16 votes from Taft to Eisenhower, when each needed every possible vote.

Dewey's omnipresence as a candidate was reflected in this chronology:

1938—nominated for Governor and almost was elected.
1940—ran for the Republican nomination for President, went to the national convention with 370 delegates, more than anyone else, but faded rapidly when the battle polarized around Robert A. Taft and Wendell L. Willkie.
1942—nominated for Governor and was elected.
1944—nominated for President and lost to Roosevelt.
1946—renominated and reelected Governor.
1948—nominated for President and lost to Truman.
1950—renominated and reelected Governor.
1952—masterminded the nomination of Eisenhower for President on the Republican ticket.
1958—played a leading role in getting the Republicans to accept Nelson Rockefeller as their candidate for Governor.

Even when Dewey left the governorship at the end of 1954, he stayed the most influential Republican in the state. The reasons for this were in the new power base he had established for himself in the Eisenhower administration in Washington where Dewey men ran the Departments of Justice, State and Treasury. His influence carried on, even in 1966, into the Lindsay Administration of City Hall. His connections maintained him as the manipulator of Republican policies in the city and state, and were also hardly a drawback in the practice of corporation law on Wall Street.

Dewey had two major asets in his role as boss rather than candidate. The first, already mentioned, was the reputation for keeping his word. He discovered very early in the political arena that this won respect from the political pros, and he followed it in practice. He even kept his word to his Lieutenant Governor, Joe Hanley, who despised Dewey as much as Dewey despised him. When Hanley withdrew as a rival for the governorship, he was promised a state sinecure for himself, and for other members of the family. Even after Hanley's letter setting forth those pledges was published under circumstances designed to hurt Dewey, he kept his word, appointing all the Hanleys to all the sinecures as soon as the election was over.

A second asset was that Dewey did not care whether another politician liked him or not; he didn't care if the politician had previously opposed him or sneered at him. If he needed the man, and the man was willing to come to terms, nothing else mattered. He enrolled many valuable lieutenants in that manner.

He reminded some of another political boss of an earlier era, Lou Payn of Columbia County, who ran the GOP in the whole Hudson River Valley. Payn, coming in late to a meeting, told the other leaders who were awaiting his word, the name of the man he planned to run for Congress.

One of them aghast, said:

"Lou, isn't he the man you've been going up and down the district calling a blankety blank son of a bitch?"

Payn answered:

"I just spent two hours with him—that's why I was late—and from now on he's *my* blankety blank son of a bitch."

## EDWARD J. FLYNN

There was not a trace of rags to riches in the saga of The Bronx boss. At the age when other political leaders had worked as bartenders or plumbers' assistants, Ed Flynn, a college graduate, was finishing law school and preparing for practice as an attorney. His career seemed set, with talent and a liking for the law, and the burgeoning Bronx as his home field of operations. The territory knew his father as a prosperous and popular general practitioner of medicine and there were many other relatives widely and favorably known.

Young Flynn was handsome, and depending on his mood exhibited a warm smile, a diffident manner and a hot temper, which is why he never thought of himself as a potential politician. But others did. In his own neighborhood a segment of the political machine in the newly created Bronx County was engaged in a fight for its life in a primary election. Its leaders felt that young Flynn, as a nominee for Assemblyman, would be an attractive addition to the ticket. He allowed himself to be persuaded and won the nomination and the election.

After three carefree years in the Legislature, he was ready to quit Albany and politics but again he was drafted to save the organization's skin. This time it was to run in the primary for Sheriff, an office in which Flynn couldn't have had less interest, but which controlled the patronage that the warring factions sought. A few months after he took office, the Bronx County leader died. Flynn was selected by Murphy of Tammany Hall to be one of a triumvirate to run what was in essence Tammany's Bronx satellite machine. Flynn, committed to support a friend who really wanted the leadership, protested his own inclusion, but Murphy's word was law. It was only when Flynn found that the triumvirate wouldn't work, that the other two were giving him the runaround that he let go with his fiery temper and told Murphy what he thought of the whole setup. The next he knew, Murphy who liked his spunk and thinking, had arranged for him to be the leader. That happened in 1922 and he was still the leader at his death in 1953.

Flynn had so little interest in the routine of politics either as a way of life or of promoting himself that he created a machine he could operate by remote control. Instead of weekly meetings with his district leaders, who bored him to death, he had the secretary of the organization set up a card index file that listed the jobs available, the performance at the polls of each district, and the amount of patronage the district rated. It took Flynn out of the back-slapping business. He just set the rules and his lieutenants carried them out. He was a firm believer in patronage, especially jobs for district leaders, on the theory that a district leader with a payroll job had less excuse for thievery. He even kept the Republican leaders on the public payroll so that they would have no incentive to head real opposition. He stressed promotion within the organization so that the alderman or assemblyman who hoped to be a magistrate would work harder and with complete loyalty if there was an established path he could tread.

He demanded and obtained a District Attorney's office run on the level with no fixes for criminals. Each successive Bronx District Attorney in his time compiled a good record and having done so was systematically promoted to the Supreme Court and several went from there to the Appellate Division.

Few had any incentive to fight the Flynn machine. Years later, long after he was dead, the Reform Movement in The Bronx was handicapped by not being able to get well-known Bronxites to lead or join them. Most were satisfied members of the old organization.

Flynn made a great deal of money out of his law practice. When he went into partnership with his boyhood friend, Monroe Goldwater, shortly after he became the Bronx leader. Both felt they had the makings of a successful political law firm, with Flynn to bring in the clients and Goldwater to do most of the courtroom work. But they also agreed politics was an uncertain business, nothing to count on in the long run for a steady living.

Political law firms were accustomed to accepting fees for allowing their names to appear on briefs while another firm did the work. The lawyers with an "in" might get $10,000, those who did the work, $40,000. Flynn and Goldwater combined the operation, insisting on using their skill as well as their "in," to collect the entire $50,000. This was a rule of the firm that never changed. It increased their income, built up the law end of the business and took them out of the realm of crass influence-peddling.

Flynn had a basic contempt for petty graft. This made it all the more ironic when he was pilloried in the newspapers for his part in the "paving block scandal." Flynn had a summer estate at Mahopac, in Putnam County. He went up one

86

weekend to find that an inner yard had been paved with several hundreds of dollars worth of city paving blocks, installed by laborers from the Bronx Borough President's office on city time. Mrs. Flynn had called the city office to ask where she could get some paving blocks, and a gallant deputy had told her he would take care of the matter, which he did, including unrequested delivery and installation.

Flynn hied himself to City Hall to tell his tale of woe to Mayor La Guardia; to find out how he could pay for the blocks and the labor. La Guardia, anxious to be helpful, made arrangements that involved doctoring the time records of the employees. In the course of this, the story of Flynn's paving blocks was leaked to the press by a La Guardia aide acting independently of his superior.

Flynn stayed mute, for the last thing a man in politics could do would be to plead innocence and pass the buck to his wife.

One reason La Guardia courted Flynn was that the Bronx boss stood high in the councils of the Roosevelt New Deal— was an intimate of the President himself. Flynn and Jim Farley were theoretically coequals as the political lieutenants of Roosevelt, but in the White House or at Hyde Park, it was always Farley who teetered on the edge of the chair as he discussed party business with the President. Flynn, relaxed, would loll back with a highball in his hand, talking business only when it was necessary to do so.

Flynn did love the big deals in politics, the settling of things of scope. It was he who was given, by Roosevelt, the delicate— and impossible—task of selling the party leaders from all over the nation the nomination of Harry S. Truman for Vice-President in 1944, without disclosing that it was the President's wish. When the others overrode him and chose James F.

Byrnes, Flynn had to bring them to the telephone to hear from Roosevelt's own lips that he wanted the man from Missouri.

In the late 1940's, the Democratic party was being hurt by a name-calling split between Mrs. Roosevelt and Francis Cardinal Spellman of New York over the principles of a federal bill for aid to education. Flynn flew secretly to Rome for a conference with Pope Pius XII, whom he had met previously as Eugenio, Cardinal Pacelli. The fruits of the trip were that the New York Cardinal paid a courtesy call on Mrs. Roosevelt at Hyde Park, the unspoken apology was publicized, and the controversy was buried.

If Flynn had a weakness as a political leader it lay in his congenital absenteeism from the job. He preferred a weekend in Kentucky, where he bred horses on a stock farm, or a prolonged party with important drinking. His tendency to let things run by themselves increased as he learned from the doctors that he had a bad heart and not very long to live. More and more he let Monroe Goldwater be his political agent—and Goldwater was a competent one—but he groomed no one interested in the Bronx leadership. When he died, the leadership passed to Charles A. Buckley, a much lower-level Flynn lieutenant, who carried out Flynn's orders competently, but on his own acted as if New York was still at the turn of the century.

## VITO MARCANTONIO

Marc was the product of the East Harlem ghetto, which he retained as his political base after his influence had spread far beyond its borders. Short, slight, shabby in dress, he was a man of many facets. To his constituents he was a friend, the first with a helping hand for anyone in need or trouble. To La Guardia, whose local political clientele he inherited, he was a son whose failings were recognized but forgiven, even indulged. To organization politicians, he was the boss of Harlem Republicans and Democrats alike, while peddling American Labor party support on a city-wide scale. To the underworld, he was both its intimate and protector. To the newspaper reader at large, he was a Congressman with an unbroken record of identification with the Communist party line.

These evaluations were all correct, but there was one common omission. In his sordid political dealings in a sordid era, he remained poor and money-honest. All he craved was power.

The people of East Harlem were the first to give it to him. The mixed Itailan and Jewish population was, in 1934, poor by even the standards of a depression-ravaged New York. It had consistently elected La Guardia to Congress, except in the Roosevelt landslide year of 1932, when the Republican line on the ballot was bad even for Fiorello. The people elected Marc the same way, again with one exception—the Landon debacle of 1936. La Guardia had attracted them by running errands and serving their needs. Marc followed the same track but was also able to mobilize the new social services, such as home relief, for which almost everyone there was eligible, and later rent controls, which applied without exception to the shoddy tenements. The voters found no reason but to hail and hero-worship Marc as they had Fiorello. Immigration of poor Puerto Ricans, displacing the Jews, even helped, as he found new voters to aid and comfort.

La Guardia gave Marc more than his old Congressional mantle. The little Mayor was a political sophisticate who had rubbed elbows with the gunmen, the gamblers, the policy-slip operators and the loan sharks of East Harlem. He knew the power these types had in any ghetto. Whatever steps he took to curtail their operations elsewhere, in Harlem he turned the handling of them over to Marc. His object was to build up Marc's political security; his method was simply to instruct the police brass to take their orders from Marc.

Underworld protection had traditionally come from Tammany district leaders in return for manpower at the polls and cash on the barrelhead, in all the years that Tammany could issue orders to the police. Marc passed up the cash and farmed out the protection franchise to those—and only those—Tammany and Republican district leaders who were willing, in return, to support him politically. He had, in this manner, the power to make or break Harlem's major party district leaders. And so his empire grew.

Marc had started out as a Republican, wearing its label successfully in 1934, futilely in 1936. By 1938, he wore the ALP tag as well, repeating in 1940. By 1942, Tammany's local representatives had come to terms with him, so he ran merrily for Congress against no opposition at all. Tom Curran, the Republican county boss, had ordered his local people to reject Marc because of his adherence to the Communist line, but the leaders, who were Marc's middlemen in the protection business, thumbed their noses. Marc was not seriously opposed at the polls by the local Republicans until the 1946 campaign, or by the Democrats until 1950. Then a three-party combination of Republicans, Democrats and Liberals behind a single opposing candidate resulted in Marc's retirement from Congress.

In addition to the open or covert support given him by the major party district leaders, he benefitted from disciplined cadres trooped into Harlem by the Communists. The Communists, with possibly 50,000 dedicated supporters, were unimportant in a state or city-wide general election, but they were very important when:

—massed within the American Labor party, at either a primary election or a membership meeting

—consolidated behind candidates for the City Council under the system of proportional representation, which fostered bullet voting, that is, casting only one first choice vote for a single candidate and ignoring all others, and

—invading a particular area of the city, where an imported Communist membership could furnish party workers as well as votes for any single candidate selected.

Marc had gone into the ALP as La Guardia had, once it was formed in 1936. Unlike La Guardia, he allied himself completely with the Communist infiltrators, and rose, with their help, to the title of State Chairman of the ALP, after the Liberals pulled out. His record in support of the Communist line was perfect. It can best be illustrated by noting that before Hitler invaded Russia (and the American Communists opposed war), Marc headed the anti-war American Peace Mobilization. When Hitler struck at Russia, and the American Communists switched to demanding war and an immediate Second Front, Marc headed the American People's Mobilization for war. His congressional votes matched.

There is much reason to believe that Marc was never a convinced Communist, that his marriage with them was one of convenience; that if Fascism had been popular in his district, he would have led the band playing "Giovanezza." But it certainly was convenient for both. With his aid, straight Communists like Benamin J. Davis, Jr. were elected to the City Council.

He joined with the Communists in giving Adam Clayton Powell, Jr. his start in Congress from the adjoining Harlem district, and after La Guardia left office as Mayor, established a close alliance with Mayor Bill O'Dwyer. He stayed palsy-walsy with Bert Stand and Clarence Neal, the two men who ran Tammany Hall during the 1940's behind several titular leaders. But the acceleration of the Cold War between America and the world Communists eventually made Marc, with his Communist affiliations, too expensive a luxury politically even for Tammany, especially since he could not give as much in return as he had in the past.

It was possible that he split genuinely with the Communists at the end, for in the 1953's mayoralty primary between Wagner and Impellitteri, he made a private call to a Wagner agent, tipping him off to a Communist maneuver designed to hurt Wagner. If the purpose was to ingratiate himself in a new area, it failed. He died, poor and out of politics, in 1954, just twenty years after his first election to Congress.

## ALEX ROSE

Rushing a small force to the right place at the right time to hit a weak spot in the ranks of the opposing army was a favorite tactic of Nathan Bedford Forrest, the Confederate cavalry leader. He characterized his method as "getting there fustest with the mostest."

Alex Rose came straight out of Forrest's handbook. Rose's political battalions were always less numerous than the rank and file of the major parties, yet he succeeded in making his followers, first in the American Labor party and then in the Liberal party, important in determining the result of elections over a thirty-year period.

Unlike other political bosses, Rose was not native-born. He came here as a fifteen-year-old, sent by well-to-do Polish parents to complete his education. The outbreak of World War I, a year later, cut him off from his family and the funds they had allocated to send him through college. He went to work in the millinery trade, joined the union, and a decade later was one of its officers. In union politics and union organizing, he showed a talent for maneuvering within the framework, developing the technique of the bluff and counter-bluff, pushing first to the strike threat and then to the peace pact. It was experience that served him well when he and the other labor leaders who outranked him took their unions into the field of partisan politics.

His first role was as Executive Director and State Secretary in 1936 of the new American Labor party. Its first nominations were Franklin D. Roosevelt for a second term as President and Herbert H. Lehman for a third term as Governor. A year later it was showing its indifference to permanent ties with the Democrats by nominating La Guardia for a second term as Mayor, and endorsing enough Republican candidates for the 1938 state constitutional convention to give the GOP control of that body. The constitutional convention endorsement was one wrung from Rose and his group at the behest of La Guardia, who wanted to pin reluctant Republican leaders behind his own renomination. Normally the Rose approach was to stress the "liberal" position of his group. Then he would cluck regretfully when one of the major parties wasn't liberal enough to enjoy its support in a particular campaign. A second tactic frequently put into play involved rushing in rapidly to adopt a promising candidate before either major party could act. This second approach was sometimes successful, sometimes boomeranged.

In the spring of 1949 Rose heard from a friendly news-
paperman that Franklin D. Roosevelt, Jr. was thinking of
starting a political career by running for Congress in a special election on Manhattan's West Side. Rose immediately
called young Roosevelt and guaranteed him support. When
Tammany Hall short-sightedly rejected Roosevelt's candidacy, Rose looked all the smarter, for the young man won in a
walk, polling a clear majority against Tammany, Republican
and ALP (Communist) opposition.

The same year, in the regular city-wide election, Rose
identified his group with the Wagner name by endorsing
young Robert F. Wagner, Jr., the Tammany candidate for
Borough President, while fusing with the Republicans on the
rest of the city-wide ticket. This involved some delicate foot-
work, but Rose's political nimbleness was up to the task.

Two years later, he plucked Rudolph Halley off the television screenings of the Kefauver Committee's exposes of the
underworld, and nominated him for President of the City
Council, to fill a vacancy. Halley had no previous Liberal
party association, or even activity in the field of labor organization but he had the best TV rating in town, and he won
handily against Democratic and Republican hacks.

These three local successes were offset by the long-range
effect of the Halley selection. In 1953 Rose and his group were
saddled with Halley as their obvious man for Mayor, and
yet they wanted to preserve the Wagner link. They offered
Wagner second place on a Halley-Wagner ticket they proposed to enter in both the Liberal and Democratic party primaries. The Wagner camp laughed it off, and while Rose's
relations with Wagner for the next eight years were marked
by no friction, Rose was an outsider as far as running City
Hall was involved.

But Rose was always a patient man. In the spring of 1961 he saw Wagner was finally splitting with Carmine De Sapio, and possibly with the other Democratic bosses as well. He sat down with Wagner, pledged him the Liberal party support in the election ahead, and moved slowly into the vacuum created by the departure of De Sapio. By election day, 1961, he was firmly in the driver's seat, and the four years of Wagner's third term provided insiders with the strange sight of the Liberal party leader dictating the strategy for leadership of the Democratic party.

Rose was able to do this because Wagner needed a political agent to replace De Sapio and Rose was there, willing and able. Needless to say, the Liberal party share of commissionerships and judgeships subject to the Mayor's control increased sharply.

When 1965 arrived and Wagner told Rose he intended to vacate City Hall, Rose had a problem. There wasn't another Democrat the Liberals could nominate who would be a sure winner of the Democratic primary and the Liberals could not wait until they knew. On the other hand, there was John V. Lindsay. The Republicans were panting to nominate the handsome young Congressman who, with the Liberal party support, might even win the election. Rose entered, with the Republicans, into a "full partnership" of the kind he never had been able to openly achieve with the Democrats.

One of Rose's most effective tools in advancing the fortunes of his group lay in his relations with the press. Very early in his career he discovered that there were political reporters of sound judgment who could be trusted to give disinterested advice to any news source, regardless of party. Rose became a first-class news source, quite apart from public statements. He was a first-class recounter of details of executive sessions and secret meetings to the political reporters who he trusted. He never mis-reported a meeting, but on the other hand, his viewpoint naturally got into the story more than the views of participants who declined comment.

A classic example of a Rose product was the leaking, in 1961, to a single reporter, of the decision of Wagner's to run his own complete, unbossed ticket in the Democratic primary, at a time when Wagner had not announced even his own candidacy. He did so, of course, as the Mayor's agent.

# 5. The Establishment

A few years ago *The New York Times* transferred to its local staff an experienced out-of-town reporter. The *Times* made what it considered a promotion on the basis of the depth and perception the editors had noted in his dispatches. After a few days in New York, the reporter turned to a colleague in the city news room and said:

"Tell me, what is the power base in this town?"

The other, a native New Yorker who had never heard the phrase, nevertheless caught on, and replied:

"If you mean who runs New York, the answer is nobody—and everybody."

The man from elsewhere had based his query on the experience that in other cities where he had worked, some individual, group, or segment of the community had run the show and probably always would. The "power base" could be the biggest employer or heaviest taxpayer; the founding family of the city itself; the local Chamber of Commerce; the big labor union; the political machine. It could consist of the half dozen solid citizens who had formed the habit of lunching at a reserved table in the best eating place, who discussed the affairs of the city as a matter of course, and were in a position to make things happen or unhappen. The "power base" was always somewhere, and a good reporter made it his business to identify it.

The reporter born and raised in New York based his answer on equally solid experience. He had found New York too big, too diverse, too downright complex and sprawling, for any single group to run. In New York the biggest taxpayer was the utility monopoly, which even as the biggest private employer of labor looked like a shoe-string operator alongside the city government itself, with 300,000 people on its payroll.

The power of sheer capital could never be massed, because it ran the gamut from Wall Street to the garment center. In labor, the Central Trades and Labor Council held meetings, but ran nothing, because it was the constituent unions which furnished the muscle. In religion, the Catholic Church always spoke with one voice, when it spoke, but it was the only church that did. The Protestant Council spoke for some denominations, not others; while among the Jews, every rabbi set his own policy in civic affairs.

In New York there always were individuals and groups with a continuing voice in and effect on the city's affairs, publicly or privately, that would answer to the name of The Establishment in some other city, state or nation. In New York, even The Establishment was divided into three main sectors, The VIP's, the Press, and the Civil Service hierarchy.

## THE VIP's

This first segment divided itself into two groups: the individuals and the organizations. Sometimes the individual achieved his status through an organization; sometimes it went the other way. For membership in any Establishment, anywhere, always was an ephemeral thing, with the membership rolls written in invisible ink. There were those who hoped they were considered members; others who were and never realized it. In New York, membership of either individual or organization could be determined by a single test:

If a high-placed official of government, up to his ears in a problem or task which would brook no normal interruption, accepted the telephone call his secretary told him was waiting on the line, the man or woman at the calling end was a member of or represented an organization of The Establishment. The chief tool of The Establishment in its operations was entree. It had it and it used it. To the politician and officeholder, The Establishment was too important and too helpful, to be kept waiting.

A perfect example of the value of The Establishment to an officeholder came during the period of the turnover of City Hall by the Wagner administration to the Lindsay administration. Two judges whose terms were expiring at midnight of the old year—too late for reappointment by Wagner, were temporarily under a cloud because they had sat in judgment on a case that had been prosecuted so lackadaisically that there was suspicion of a political fix. The judges were innocent. Lindsay was under pressure to reappoint them. But the cloud had to be removed. So ten days before Lindsay took office, the Bar Association, part of The Establishment, issued a report clearing them of any responsibility or fault. The new Mayor then reappointed them on the basis of the report. The Bar Association report, of course, was prearranged, not in content, but in timing, to suit the convenience and necessities of the situation as the new Mayor saw them.

Another example would involve a move by some non-Establishment group—possibly in the social welfare field—which would be pressing the city administration for action that sounded attractive, but was ill-conceived. Standard procedure would be for the administration to call in The Establishment segment operating in the same area and have it beat the drums for action along better lines, in the same area. This would produce results for public view and take the administration off the hook.

Again, the Mayor could have a candidate for a particularly important job whom he regarded as the only one for it. Rather than spring his nomination cold, without advance notice or knowledge of reaction, he would consult with The Establishment in that area, even persuade it to write letters to the newspapers, suggesting the nomination.

The Bar Association, whose mission has been noted, was only one of possibly 50 completely diverse organizations that would be accepted as owning membership in The Establishment. A casual skimming of the list would spotlight the Patrolmen's Benevolent Association, the Citizens Committee for Children, The New York Shipping Association, the Consolidated Edison Company, the Park Association, the Citizens Budget Commission, the Roman Catholic Church, and the Public Education Association, just for a start.

When it came to individuals, some who possibly best typified it did so before the phrase Establishment had been accepted into the idiom. There was Charles C. Burlingham, who lived to be more than one hundred, who was an effective force on the side of the angels for more than half a century. A spearhead of reform even before the Mitchel administration, he was the only man Fiorello La Guardia respected to the point of never losing his temper in front of him, or with him.

Burlingham, a paper saver, would scrawl important advice on a single sheet of paper, writing up and down the margins. The Mayor would reply, in complete seriousness, on the back of used envelopes.

Another was Samuel Untermyer, attorney and financier, who had investigated Wall Street and the House of Morgan for the U.S. Senate after the 1907 crash, and who in his later years was a leader in Jewish affairs and a member of the War Board of Tammany Hall. In his colorful, buccaneering career, he accumulated so much of a fortune that he could work for the city for nothing—for seven years in the late 1920's and early 1930's—protecting the then sacred five cent subway fare. His fingers were in so many political and civic pies simultaneously that any City Hall reporter worth his salt dropped down to Untermyer's Pine Street office at least once a week, for an off-the-record chat, just to keep informed.

Herbert Bayard Swope, somewhat of a free lance after he left the executive editorship of the foundering old *New York World*, felt and made others feel he had squatting rights at any conference table. When he didn't represent himself, he represented Bernard M. Baruch.

In more recent years the list included Adele Rosenwald Levy (philanthropy); Herbert H. Lehman (philanthropy and politics); Helen Hall, Mary Lasker and Trude Lash (social welfare and politics); Monroe Goldwater, Samuel I. Rosenman and Eugene V. Keogh (politics and the bar); John A. Coleman and John J. Lynch (fund-raising and the two Roman Catholic Archdioceses); Harry Van Arsdale, David Dubinsky and Louis Hollander (organized labor); and David Rockefeller (banking and real estate).

Really moneyed members of The Establishment, Mrs. Levy, Lehman, and David Rockefeller, afforded representatives,—

specialists in particular fields—who could sit in through the working out of programs which their principals had initiated, and there was no need for the principals to appear again until the culmination. This saved a lot of wear and tear.

For any city administration, the existence of the VIP section of The Establishment was a constant pain in the budget. It could practically force a pay rise for the police, commit the city to new welfare, park and hospital programs that sometimes not only cost cash in hand, but took taxable real estate off the rolls. The comfort any administration derived was that it could count on public acclaim (Establishment-inspired) for the program, and also that the members of The Establishment possessed vast money-raising talents that were at the service of the official who served them.

## THE PRESS

New York City's newspapers, despite mergers and consolidations over a forty-year period, remained numerous, were well circulated, and had outstanding prestige in their field in the state, the nation and the world. One daily had by far the largest circulation in America, another was consistently ranked as the best newspaper produced anywhere. Even those that ranked neither as the largest nor the best stood comparison with the best elsewhere, in terms of scope and quality of news coverage.

In the spring of 1966 there were 11 daily newspapers classified officially as of general circulation; 69 separate neighborhood sheets; 69 more in foreign languages, ranging from 3 in Arabic to 11 in Yiddish, and 15 specialty trade papers of the type of *Women's Wear Daily* and the *New York Law Journal*.

## The Establishment

Those that were active as part of The Establishment were *The Times, Herald Tribune* (which folded later in 1966) and *Daily News* in the morning field; the *World-Telegram & Sun, Journal-American* (now merged) and *Post* in the afternoon field, and three papers of the Newhouse chain: the *Long Island Press,* the *Star Journal* and *Staten Island Advance* with circulation in Queens and Richmond. *The Wall Street Journal* and *Journal of Commerce* stuck to finance and business and stayed out of local government and politics.

There were always many cities in America that had only one major newspaper, frequently well-edited and with prestige. The common situation would be for that newspaper to play ball consistently with the local City Hall, both in news and editorial columns, or else to fight it tooth and nail, asking and giving no favors.

In New York, the story was always somewhat different. The press sought and accepted favors from any administration in power—as its just due under the First Amendment—while it reserved complete freedom of action for itself in the editorial and news columns. It pictured itself as a dispassionate civic gadfly, against sin, partisan politics and special privilege, even while accepting the latter.

The feeling of the press that it had special rights was not a new one. As far back as 1935 the publishers fought the constitutionality of the National Labor Relations Act, opening the door for the first time to widespread union organization, not on the grounds that Congress was unconstitutionally broadening its powers over commerce, but on the basis that it enjoyed special constitutional exemption—the freedom of the press.

In New York the result was that the politicians and the officeholders never stopped courting the press, and also never avoided getting kicked in the teeth for their pains. Every public agency maintained a press officer with the primary duty of keeping the press happy. This involved supplying it with information by formal handouts, tipping reporters off unofficially to good stories in the hope of building a reservoir of good will, and arranging for special privileges for the reporters, the publishers and their friends and relations. None of these was ever worth a hoot when the paper's policy of the moment called for unfriendly attention.

The only Mayor who ever recognized even the possibility of another course was La Guardia, who while hailed as great in retrospect, took a steady beating from a portion of the press while he was still around. He argued that the only way to handle newspaper attacks was to hit the publisher in the pocketbook. He even tried it, but eventually got weary of the struggle.

Later there were episodes in support of the La Guardia theory that publisher policies could be affected by financial considerations. For example, the plaint of successive city administrations that the city was being shortchanged, in post World War II years, by Republican administrations in Albany was laughed at by the press, until Wagner sat down with the publishers and convinced them that their own tax monies were involved. The tone of coverage changed overnight.

Later, a proposed extension of the sales tax to services, such as plumbing, upholstering, auto repairs and also those rendered by newspapers and other advertising media, was blasted by every newspaper in New York until the city folded, and withdrew the measure. Five years later a similar extension of the sales tax to services, *excluding* those rendered by newspapers and other advertising media, was enacted without newspaper clamor or reference to the change.

# The Establishment

It was also uncontrovertible that police were on regular assignment to hold up ordinary traffic in front of any newspaper plant while its supply of newsprint was unloaded; that its delivery trucks enjoyed immunity from traffic tickets and use of the West Side Highway and East River Drive from which all other trucking was excluded; that friendly valuation for tax purposes of newspaper real estate was the rule rather than the exception, and that the newspaper lobby could at any time, make itself the most powerful and effective in town.

In the city's government and politics, the role of the press as part of The Establishment was to act as its eyes, ears, mouth and bulletin board.

The VIP segment would "sell" its case for a program or project to the newspaper owner, publisher, editor, city editor, or even reporter—sometimes both ends at once—to insure editorial and news coverage of developments. When it discussed its ideas with the officeholders involved, they were made rapidly aware of the fact that The Establishment case was going to get top billing and favorable treatment in the press. If the VIP's were peddling a program which the governmental powers had already privately approved, or asked it to peddle, they were equally able to insure a good press reception.

The press, once having taken a position on an issue, could not change overnight. To do so would be to acknowledge fallibility, and while errors appeared in the news columns and were corrected, that never could be true of the mature judgment of the editorial pages. Editorial attitudes could be changed only after intervals decent enough for the readers to have forgotten the earlier posture, or for a change in the underlying situation to have occurred.

## The Establishment

In the workings of The Establishment, this meant that whichever segment sold its position first as the only valid one, held the upper hand for keeps in the argument. This was a priceless advantage for those who comprehended the system. It was equally a disadvantage to any responsible public official who disliked giving in to clamor when the clamorers were all wrong.

One instance out of many—There was a site along the East River which had been rejected for low-rent public housing because it was next to a twenty-four-hour-a-day Con Edison power plant and the only access to it was through a street lined with sanitation trucks and their garage. Con Edison offered to buy the site, at a good price, to enlarge its power plant. A leading newspaper was sold a bill of goods that the land should be used for more expensive middle-income housing. Thereupon the city's decision was attacked by the newspaper on the basis of probable venality, with a listing of all the "friends" Con Edison must have had at City Hall. The reasons which made the site impossible for housing were disregarded as just alibis. It was amusing, though not pertinent, that after the city sold the site to Con Edison anyhow, it turned out to be valueless for anything but a parking lot. Once under water, it had been filled in with junk and could support foundations for neither a housing project nor a power plant.

Another editorial page was similarly "sold" a program to solve the water shortage by metering the water piped into each apartment house, on the contention that less would be wasted if paid for by the drop. The flaw in the argument lay in the fact that while some water could be saved by the landlord repairing leaks he might otherwise ignore, this could easily be counterbalanced by any tenants who would happily let the water run if they knew it cost the landlord money. When this was pointed out to the editorial pundit, he amended the program to meter each apartment.

Unfortunately, the editorial writer had always commuted to work from the suburbs and didn't know that in a city apartment house, each pipe ran from the cellar to the top floor, not through the apartment, and that to measure the water each tenant used would require a separate meter on each tap —a minimum of five meters per tenant in turn-of-the-century tenements, and two dozen or more in superior housing accommodations. The fact that subsequent recommendations for water metering by official agencies ruled out the metering of individual apartments, and most of the editorial writer's estimate of water saving, was not mentioned on that paper's editorial page.

On the other side, there were at least as many instances where editorial and news column pressures pushed government into action that was proper and that had been delayed by either inertia or cost factors.

The same newspaper which got over its head on water metering took an unfailing stand for taxes to meet the increased governmental costs it espoused in many fields. It did not live in the dreamworld that wanted increased services to be financed out of thin air.

In many other newspapers, exposure in the news columns of neglect of facilities—housing, parks, playgrounds—was warranted and brought action, though sometimes at the expense of another program just as needed, but not spotlighted.

The press remained the powerful arm of The Establishment because the people in government, jealous of their own reputations, and with full knowledge of how those could be built up or torn down, courted the newspapers with the same zeal that their campaign treasurers would welcome a contributor.

## THE CIVIL SERVICE

The vast majority of the city's 300,000 employees were represented in The Establishment by employee organizations that essentially were labor unions but whose power and influence predated collective bargaining for municipal employees.

The Civil Service system got its start with a push from Grover Cleveland at the national level and from Teddy Roosevelt in New York State. The state laws that governed the hiring and firing of both state and city employees were expanded steadily over a seventy-five year period, to cover or "bind in" more and more jobs that had belonged to political patronage under the old spoils system. The theory was that the little people in government would thus be protected against the vicissitudes of partisan politics, on the one hand, and that by competitive examination the city would gain able employees.

In time the competitive Civil Service grew to the point in numbers, and degree of organization, that it constituted one of the most potent lobbies in Albany and at City Hall. Job protection became almost absolute; pay and benefits continually improved.

Consider this dilemma:

When the Lindsay administration took over from the Wagnerites, a number of Lindsay's assistants scurried through the ranks of private enterprise to find secretaries willing to switch over to City Hall. But when it came to putting them to work, they found that the Mayor's Office was already staffed with competent, well paid (average salary $9,000) *permanent* secretaries, one or two of whom dated back even to the La Guardia administration. Under the law, the incumbents could not even be transferred out of City Hall to another agency without their own signed consents. And even if any had consented, the vacancies could have been filled only by persons who had already taken Civil Service examinations and promotion tests. These secretaries, who had achieved their rank by promotions over the years, were protected by laws the reformers always had pressed and always seemed surprised to find existed. There were many other areas of employment where union organization gave additional practical guarantees. The police and firemen's line organizations while not called unions, functioned as such.

An example:

The city had had on its books since the middle 1930's the ill-conceived Lyons residence law, passed originally to curb La Guardia's propensity to hire commissioners and experts from outside the city. The law required anyone to be hired by the city to have been a resident for at least three years prior to his employment. It also required continued residence in the city after employment. When the author of the law, Borough President James J. Lyons of the Bronx finally left office in 1961, sentiment finally jelled for repeal of the statute.

But the incumbent Police Commissioner refused to go along with a law that permitted his patrolmen to live so far away from their beats, even though the police, as well as the firemen, had flouted the restrictions for years and everybody, including the Commissioner, knew it. In return, the organized police lobby refused to accept repeal of the original residence requirement for newcomers without repeal of the section that supposedly hit the old-timers. The dilemma was resolved and the law repealed when the Police Commissioner himself quit, for other reasons, and a more reasonable successor took office. It might have been noted that it was the non-Establishment Commissioner who vanished, not the established police lobby.

Another example, with a somewhat different twist:

The Commissioner of Borough Works of Manhattan, in the days before a city Highway Department, ordered a major Manhattan avenue repaved. The street needed repaving, the Borough President's office had its own asphalt-producing plant, and it had plenty of employees to do the work. But the paver's union wanted the work done by private contractors, who employed most of its members, so it threatened to throw a picket line around every city construction project. A deal was finally hammered out whereby two thirds of each year's paving work would be done by private contract, and one third by the Borough President's men. This approximated past division of the work in dollar volume. In the background of the agreement, unstated by either side, was the fact that some of the city crew also belonged to the paver's union, and if the city-executed work was curtailed too much, those who belonged to the paver's union would be the first to be laid off, since their jobs were non-competitive, and theoretically less secure.

While the bulk of the city employees thus influenced operations of government, important influence by smaller groups also existed. They were (1) veteran employees who had reached the status of bureau or division chiefs, and for whom special titles had been created, and (2) experts in specialized fields, hired originally as such. Both held positions that were classified as "non-competitive." This meant that specifications had been set up for the jobs, and applicants, rather than taking tests, presented credentials that measured up to the technical, academic, or experience requirements stated for them. This sometimes worked the way it appeared, sometimes it did not, for the specifications could have been framed at the start to fit a particular individual.

An example:

The city's Department of Education, which had a miserable record for efficiency in school construction and maintenance, was finally persuaded to hire a first-rate man for the top job. He had successfully superintended the same area for the Roman Catholic Archdiocese. After he had been in office for several months and was obviously making a success of the operation, it developed that he did not meet the job specifications drawn to fit his predecessors and was not therefore legally qualified to hold the post. The fact that he was practically qualified—as his predecessors had shown themselves not to be—didn't matter in the eye of the Civil Service law. Fortunately, the job was one that was in the sphere of public consciousness, and the ouster of the incumbent on grounds so ludicrous generated enough pressure for a change in the specifications and the elimination of some academic requirements never pertinent to it in the first place.

The field of "experts" was a newcomer to the categories of public employment, and stemmed from a public and editorial page demand that in hospitals, social welfare, smoke control, education, etc. the administrative and even policy-making jobs be filled by persons who were experts in the field. It got its big start in New York in the office of the City Administrator —a post in itself created to meet half-way the arguments for a technical city manager, who would run the city in a manner completely divorced from politics.

As it turned out, partisan politics was to a large extent

eliminated. It remained questionable whether equally political motivation, on a less identifiable basis, had also been eliminated.

The department would hire a top man on the basis of qualifications drawn for the city by an agency with a reputation in the field. He would set the qualifications for his staff and his assistants. These would, in effect, be written into the law by their adoption by the Municipal and State Civil Service Commissions. As time wore on, it became apparent that there were many elements of self-promotion involved within an informal "experts' union."

Just as the Communists had infiltrated government in the early 1930's, and hired, promoted and recommended one another, so did those active in many fields of expertise when that became fashionable in government in the late 1950's and early 1960's.

Since the city was committed to the employment of experts, it had to take their advice, or fire them for incompetence which was silly on the face of it, since they fitted the job descriptions written for them, and would have been judged for their competence by their accomplices. An administration that turned a policy question over to the "experts" for report found, more often than not, that the basic recommendation always called for the hiring of more experts.

This was Parkinson's Law at work, a new segment of The Establishment entrenching itself with no noticeable increase in services and productivity, but definitely reflected in administrative expense.

# 6. Race, Color or Creed

New York is unique politically because it has not been a city with one identifiable and important minority—it is composed of a great complex of minorities, each of which had to fight first for existence and later for equality.

Emphasis all over America in the past decade has been on wiping out discrimination based on color. New York, pioneer in so many things, passed its first state Civil Rights law in 1895, at the demand of the city people. The law prohibited denial of accommodations in theaters, restaurants, hotels—all public places—based on race, color, creed or *country of national origin*.

The white immigrant of the period of 1850 to 1920 dominated the politics of the city with little concern over color until he had to make room for the later-arriving southern Negro and the Puerto Rican.*

New York, rather than Boston, or Philadelphia or Balti-

---

* The 1960 census, giving the city's total population as 7,781,000, grouped 3,785,000 first and second generation Americans as of "foreign stock," with the principal countries of origin being Ireland, 311,-000; Germany, 324,000; Poland, 389,000; USSR, 563,000 and Italy

more, had become the natural port of entry for a young prospective American. The completion of the Erie Canal, in 1825, added the advantage of an access route to the interior, to the formidable asset the city already possessed in its great landlocked harbor for the sailing vessel.

The immigrants from Europe poured into and through the city by the millions every decade. Many went West to populate metropolises-to-be such as Pittsburgh, Chicago, St. Louis or Milwaukee. Others, when they stepped thankfully off the ship, settled where they landed.

Racial overtones in the politics of the community are not unique to New York City. In far-off Minnesota, haven of the Scandinavians, a factor in the election contest between candidate Andersen and Anderson would be the regional Scandinavian distinction involved in spelling the last syllable.

It has been equally commonplace to note the German vote in Milwaukee, the Irish vote in South Boston, or the Negro vote of Chicago's South Side, single identifiable minority groups of political import.

In New York—if we ignore the American Indian—the so-called original settlers were Protestant Nordics—the Dutch and English. Though they still own a great deal of the city, and live handsomely off it, they have been inundated politically by the great immigration waves before the twentieth century.

The 1895 enactment noted at the beginning of this chapter, reflected the political enterprise of the Irish who started coming in the late 1840's and continued in great numbers. By the

---

858,000. The great flow of European immigrants dropped off to a trickle forty years earlier, as a result of restrictive legislation, and the third generation descendants of the earlier Irish, Jewish and Italian arrivals are classified officially as "native Americans of native stock." The same census listed 1,116,000 as "non-white" and 612,000 as Puerto Ricans.

1890's, they were down at the piers to meet the Jews and Italians and enroll them as citizens and Democrats. Any office seeker of this day who can afford the price of a European vacation automatically plays the Three-I Circuit, visiting Ireland, Italy and Israel impartially. It gives him that current, informal identification so easily dropped into a speech—"the last time I was in . . ." with the country determined by the makeup of his audience.

On the other hand, it should be made perfectly clear that there is no Irish, Italian or Jewish vote to be counted on by a candidate for major office simply because he belongs to that minority. Attempts to secure votes that way have backfired as often as not. Roosevelt, Harriman, Dewey, Rockefeller and Lindsay, all white Protestants, could and did get votes from each of the other, far larger, minorities. There is no absolute allegiance by any of the important minorities that either major party can depend on for a specific election. With knowledge of this, party leaders evaluate prospective candidates in the light of the issues of the particular year, and the election that follows is waged along the lines so drawn.

Robert F. Wagner, Sr., born in Germany, came up for reelection as United States Senator both in 1938 and 1944, when Nazi Germany was the total enemy of every New York Jew. But there was never the slightest question about Wagner's renomination or reelection, because the New York Jews were expected to, and did, vote for Wagner on his New Deal record. On the other hand, in 1933, at the very start of Hitler's regime, when it developed that an Irish candidate for Mayor had penned, two decades earlier, something that could be stretched by interpretation as anti-Semitic, this became a powerful weapon against him and probably encompassed his defeat.

Jacob Javits, a Jew, won his first reelection to the House of

Representatives from a predominantly Jewish-Irish-Democratic upper Manhattan district, on the Republican ticket because the Irish Democrats of the area thought Javits' Democratic opponent was leftish.

The continued and continuing group identification of aspirants for office, and officeholders themselves, is not necessarily demagogic in motive. It stems more from the parochialism mandated by the size of the city. A man can't get ahead just because he is known favorably by his neighbors. He must achieve a reputation within a segment of the city to be presentable to all of it.

The ambitious or even just public-spirited citizen becomes active in good causes and charity drives. He joins the lodge of a brotherhood, which usually has a racial or religious orientation. He heads a settlement house committee, raises funds for a summer camp or hospital endowment. If a Jew, he rises high in the Federation of Jewish Philanthropies. As a Catholic, he is honored by membership on the Cardinal's Committee of the Laity, or even by knighthood in the papal orders of Malta or St. Gregory. The Italians have their Columbian Society. Every race, color and creed has its own list of charitable or just plain chowder and marching societies, identifying the membership background even unto the third and fourth generation.

The city is so big that the political animal who doesn't identify with his own race suffers the dual handicap of losing his own, and attracting no others. Actually, a candidate who isn't counted on to bring in the support of at least his own kind, isn't nominated in the first place.

The New York Jews, least clannish of the major groups when it comes to voting, were for the Protestant Franklin Roosevelt en masse because he was a friend. Yet let a progenitor of their blood like the turn-of-the-century Nathan Straus—or a later Herbert Lehman—win fame as a philanthropist, and the family name is good for votes unto the grandchildren. Equally, in the case of a recent candidate nominated to appeal to the "Jewish vote," the research on the part of the nominators was poor and the fact that he had married outside his religion and that *his* wealthy family had not been noted for philanthropy proved disastrous among the largest Jewish voting group in the world. They voted for his Protestant Republican opponent.

The crosscurrent of race and religion in New York can raise havoc even with the statistician, as one of them discovered.

In the late 1930's, there was a City Council investigation of home relief administration that usually is recalled only for having brought the word "boondoggle" into the general vocabulary. The investigating committee held countless hearings and issued innumerable reports, one of which listed relief recipients by religious affiliation.

There was an immediate challenge of the accuracy of the figures by the Roman Catholic Church, conveyed by an authorized layman to the committee chairman. There just weren't that many Catholics on relief, the Cardinal's Irish spokesman contended. The committee chairman opened the books for inspection, and after only a few moments, the emissary from the Cathedral said:

"I see where the discrepancy is. You've counted in the Italians."

The church changed its attitude markedly in the years that followed, being first, for example, among the religious denominations to welcome the Puerto Rican newcomers.

Much more discerning were the remarks of Al Smith in

1934, when in the role of senior statesman, he attended a small, intimate dinner devoted to raising funds for the relief of Jews in Germany.

"All my life," said Smith, "I've been hearing about the plight of the poor Jews, some place in the world. It used to be the persecuted Jews in Russia, or the poor Jews in Poland, or the starving Jews in Armenia. Now it's the Jews in Germany.

"As I look around the room tonight, I see the Governor here, Herby Lehman. He's Jewish. Take the Mayor, (La Guardia) he's half Jewish. The President of the Board of Aldermen, my old job, Bernie Deutsch, he's Jewish, and so is Sam Levy, the Borough President of Manhattan. I'm beginning to wonder if someone shouldn't do something for the poor Irish, here in New York."

It would be difficult to pose a better introduction to the status in New York of the major voting groups.

## THE IRISH

New York City's Irish voters were, for decades, the most steadfast supporters of the Democratic party at the polls, sticking to its emblem in good years and bad. In recent times their allegiance has become shaky.

The Irish became Democrats when they first came here in numbers in the 1840's, and found themselves looked down upon by an existing Establishment ruled by Protestant Whigs, later Protestant Republicans. The innately rebellious Irishmen set out to do something about it, and by the time of the consolidation of 1897, they were solidly entrenched in the Democratic party and had complete control of Tammany Hall. In those days an Irish Republican was as socially acceptable as a white integrationist in Mississippi in the early 1960's.

There was an unbroken succession of Irish leaders of Tammany Hall from the days of Croker who was boss at the formation of the Greater City until 1948. There was the same span of Irish leadership in the other counties within the city. At first, the election of Irish to major public office was limited by discretion. To appease or court the voting blocs of Protestant Scandinavians, Germans and English in Brooklyn, the Irish leadership nominated Protestants for Mayor, electing all but one, until John Purroy Mitchel, the first Catholic Mayor, was put into office by Tammany's Fusion opposition in 1913.

From then on, keeping their unchallenged control of the party machinery, the Irish moved with new drive into the field of elective office. By 1926, at the start of the Walker administration, the Board of Estimate, the city's governing body, consisted of six Irish Catholics—the Mayor, Controller, President of the Board of Aldermen, the Borough Presidents of Kings, Queens and Richmond. The Borough President of Manhattan was a Jew, of The Bronx, a German. They furnished the political leadership, solid and stable in Murphy's time, narrow and stupid in many of the later years. The election of Al Smith as Governor, and his tremendous prestige in that office, rubbed off and shone on the Irish political machine.

Since the end of the Mitchel regime, every Democratic candidate for Mayor has been an Irish Catholic with the exception of Ferdinand Pecora, Protestant Italian, in 1950, Abraham D. Beame, Jewish, in 1965, and Robert F. Wagner, only half-Irish but all Catholic, in 1953, 1957 and 1961.

The domination of the party machine, from the highest echelon down to the district leader and the precinct captain, gave the Irish the greatest bread and butter stake in the party's success. They voted the ticket, straight, because city jobs, favors and their own prestige were involved.

The reasons for the later Irish wanderlust are complicated. They could be captioned "England," "Roosevelt" and "Communism," with a subtitle, "The Dispossessed."

The first Irish revolt against the Democrats was early, and at the time, an isolated phenomenon. In 1919, with the League of Nations being set up to govern the affairs of the world, the demands for Irish freedom from English bondage were shouted as loud in New York as in Dublin. Daniel P. Cohalan, a pillar of Tammany, who spoke with a deep brogue, though born in Orange County, New York, quarreled publicly with President Woodrow Wilson because Wilson had not fought hard enough for, and obtained, a free and independent Ireland. Most of New York's Irish agreed with Cohalan.

In the local election that fall, the Irish bolted the Democratic ticket en masse. They voted Republican, with the result that Fiorello H. La Guardia, later Tammany's bête noire, was elected to the city-wide post of President of the Board of Aldermen; a similar vacancy in the Presidency of the Borough of Manhattan was filled by a Republican, and even Republican judicial candidates running for what normally would have been the exercise, found themselves elected.

There was a long hiatus. With Al Smith in Albany, or running for President, with Jimmy Walker following Red Mike Hylan into City Hall, the Irish felt Democratic and politically secure. The next desertion of the Democratic ticket came in 1936. Herbert H. Lehman, the Jewish Democratic Governor, had vetoed a Catholic Church supported measure for the public transportation of parochial school children in school buses at the legislative session in the spring, and the Republicans sought to capitalize on it by nominating an Irish

Republican as Lehman's opponent. The result was that Lehman trailed Roosevelt by half a million in his New York City plurality.

As World War II in Europe approached, many of the Irish, still hating England, became isolationists in their thinking. And as the President, Roosevelt, acted more and more like a friend of England, the Irish regarded him less and less as one of their own, Democrat or not. In the 1940 Presidential election, though Roosevelt carried New York City by a whopping majority, a number of the Irish-populated Assembly districts voted Republican, even down to local office.

Divorces among the many Roosevelt children, the public quarrel between Mrs. Roosevelt and Cardinal Spellman over a federal aid-to-education bill, were added factors that alienated Irish Democrats from the Roosevelt tradition. One of the sub-surface factors in Harry Truman's surprise retention of the presidency in 1948 was the temporary return of the Irish to the Democratic party, now that they no longer had to vote for Roosevelt as its standard-bearer. Truman did lose New York State by 61,000 votes, but this was not the doing of the Irish, but of 500,000 others who voted for Henry Wallace's leftish Progressive party candidacy.

Then there was "Communism." The uncompromising opposition of the Catholic Church to Red Russia, stilled for purpose of national welfare during World War II, broke out in full force when Russia confirmed the Church's worst beliefs, and started the Cold War. The word "Yalta" was an epithet among New York's Irish before Joe McCarthy was heard of. In the 1946 state and congressional elections, the Catholics virtually led the nation in going Republican. In the McCarthy era, encompassing the last two years of Truman and the first two years of Eisenhower in the White House, the Irish were heavily pro-McCarthy, and showed it at the polls. Adlai Stevenson had absolutely no appeal to them. The Democrats might even have been in trouble on the mayoralty in 1953 if the party nominee had not been Wagner, accepted as one of them by the Irish, and welcome also to the Jews for his social welfare background.

The final factor, the feeling of being dispossessed from what had been their party, is a many-pronged one, developed over the years. First, they had had to yield their undisputed control of the party machinery and share it first with the Jews and Italians, and later with the Negroes. They no longer parcelled out, but shared, the nominations to the legislature and the bench. They yielded district leaderships and public jobs. Finally, even the top-ranking leadership of Tammany Hall and the Brooklyn organization.

Secondly, the Irish party workers, the grass roots organizer for the ticket, who once had brought dozens of votes to the polls with clockwork regularity, and was rewarded with minor public office, lost importance and eventually quit. He was removed from his niche in politics by the public assistance programs that replaced the party handout, and competitive Civil Service gradually took away his one-time public payroll sinecure.

Thirdly, the "socialization of government" to which the Democratic party had been committed was linked by many of the Irish dissidents with the advent of Southern Negroes and Puerto Ricans in neighborhoods that the Irish had settled originally and felt they still owned. Mass pressure from the newcomers displaced the third generation Irish from large areas of Manhattan's middle West Side, Chelsea, Hell's Kitchen and lower Yorkville. Many of them moved to the suburbs, others to Queens.

Originally, when the Irish started leaving the Democratic

party in state and national elections because they felt it had left them, they retained party standing in their own minds by continuing to vote Democratic for Mayor. In the 1965 mayoralty election, however, most informed observers felt that the Irish vote cast for William F. Buckley, the Conservative party nominee, who campaigned by voicing their discontent, was one of the major factors in the defeat of Beame, the Democratic nominee.

## THE JEWS

New York's Jewish immigrants did not marry the Democratic party as soon as they landed, the way their Irish predecessors had done. The affiliation that exists today followed a long period of courtship in which voters of Jewish faith or background flirted with and were sought after by both major parties. In the early years, the Jews were even more attracted to, and active in, the old Socialist party.

The breed of socialism they went for was basically that of the European trade unions with which they have lived or heard about. It stressed labor rights, government ownership or regulation of natural resources, public utilities and general means of production, etc. The Socialist platform of 1900 had been taken over almost in toto by the Democrats by 1936, and by the Republicans, with greater reluctance, a few years later.

This Jewish interest in issues of social reform helped moved them into the Democratic party, slowly starting in the days of Al Smith, and much more rapidly with the advent of Franklin D. Roosevelt's New Deal. In presidential elections, the New York Jewish businessman, and even his employees, were likely to vote Republican, up to 1932, on the theory that the Republican party was "good for business." On local issues, identification with the majority Democratic party was considerable, but individual, rather than en masse.

By the middle 1960's, the Jews had become the largest identifiable group within the city, extremely vote-conscious, and with their attitude toward a particular candidate frequently the decisive one, though they were overwhelmingly Democrats in enrollment and normal voting tendencies.

In 1900, New York, with just about half the people the 1960 census takers counted, housed about 400,000 Jews whose influence on city politics was minimal. Living in a world of their own, were the wealthy German Jewish families who had emigrated in Europe's troubled year of 1848, or had moved up from the southern United States following the Civil War. The list included names like Straus, Schiff, Warburg, Morgenthau, Guggenheim, Lewisohn and Lehman, important then as today in the fields of trade and finance. Some of them contributed money to political activities, but only in the line of business. They did not participate themselves.

Down below were the non-English speaking Russian and Polish Jews, who read the Yiddish newspapers and trudged off at daybreak from the lower East Side tenements to do piecework in the garment trade sweatshops. Over the decades, they learned English, educated their children, spread out into Brooklyn and The Bronx with the expanded rapid transit lines, while an upper middle class that came into being through ownership of garment industry firms, moved into prestige addresses on Manhattan's West End Avenue and Riverside Drive, or the new Bronx Grand Concourse.

Their tendency to vote Socialist died slowly. Even today New York's Liberal party, as close a successor as any to the old Socialist group, attracts more Jews as members than any other group. In Brooklyn's Brownsville, where the working-class Jews formed a majority of the electorate, the Democrats and Republicans had to combine on occasion, prior to 1920, to defeat the Socialist nominees. And the same happened once or twice in the area of the Jewish Plymouth Rock, the lower East Side. They polled, in the 1917 mayoralty election, a vote big enough to finish third in a five-man race.

In 1918 they elected five members of the State Assembly, only to see those men denied their seats on the grounds that they were dangerous radicals by the upstate Republican witch-hunters of the post World War I era.

Al Smith's battle against the unseating of the Socialist Assemblymen helped dramatize Smith as a liberal in the eyes of the liberal-minded New York Jew. His switch to the Democratic party for particular candidates became more frequent. There had been other, earlier attractions.

Tammany Hall virtually earmarked the office of the Borough President of Manhattan as the principal elective office with which to recognize the Jews politically. Except for the four years from 1917 to 1921, the Borough President of Manhattan was of the Jewish faith, starting with Marcus M. Marks in 1909 and ending only with the election of Robert F. Wagner, Jr., in 1949. Parenthetically, this particular earmarking had become unnecessary by then, since Jews were recognized with city-wide nominations as early as 1933, and had already begun developing a stake in party politics and the political machinery previously monopolized by the Irish.

Woodrow Wilson won much personal support with his tremendously controversial appointment of Louis D. Brandeis, both labor lawyer and Jew, to the United States Supreme Court. The social legislation that followed the Factory Investigating Committee, the later reliance by Governor Al Smith on Jewish advisers such as Belle Moskowitz and Joseph

M. Proskauer, led the working-class Jew to feel he had friends among the Democrats.

This empathy with the Democrats was vastly increased in the Roosevelt era. The New Deal had a philosophic appeal to the Jews from the outset, and FDR's later leadership of the world opposition to Hitler cemented the ties. The New York City Jews contributed substantially to the city majorities needed to overcome upstate Republican voting not only for Roosevelt every time he ran, but for Truman and later John F. Kennedy. Their votes for Stevenson were of no avail. Barry Goldwater, even with a set of Jewish grandparents, had no appeal in New York City at all.

The Jews cannot be counted on to be Democrats en masse, but there are certain predictable patterns. Democratic and Republican Jews will unite to smite anti-Semitism. In 1938, for example, New York City Republican Jews cut the Republican state ticket because one of Tom Dewey's running mates used a campaign slogan that they thought had an anti-Semitic flavor, and the vote was so close for the head of the ticket that this factor may have decided the election in favor of the Democratic incumbent, Herbert Lehman.

The Democratic Jews will vote overwhelmingly for a Democratic Jew they regard as truly representative of their race, like Lehman, and in substantial numbers even for a Republican, Jacob Javits. But they won't vote for a candidate on either ticket just because he is a Jew. Examples include the failure of Albert Ottinger to make inroads into the Jewish Democratic voters in his 1928 gubernatorial race against Franklin D. Roosevelt, who ran on Al Smith's ticket; the poor race of Jonah J. Goldstein, Republican-Liberal nominee for Mayor against William O'Dwyer, on the Democratic-American Liberal party tickets, in 1945; and the 1962 gubernatorial candidacy of Robert Morgenthau, that was publicized by the press as a contrived bid for the Jewish vote that had gone to Nelson Rockefeller four years earlier. Rockefeller got it the second time, too.

Finally, an element of faddism is definitely detectable in the voting tendencies of the increasingly large group of upper-middle class Jews. Having gone hook, line and sinker for Adlai Stevenson, they at first resented John F. Kennedy's candidacy as depriving Stevenson of a third Presidential nomination. They voted for Kennedy on Election Day, mostly out of preferring him to Richard M. Nixon. They became tremendously enthusiastic about Kennedy later, after he was President. After the assassination, they reverted to their original dislike for the Kennedy family, voting against his brother, Robert, in favor of Keating, a candidate who otherwise had no special appeal and who turned out to be a loser anyhow.

In 1958, they bolted Averell Harriman, whom they had elected in 1954, in favor of the fresher face and even better known name of Nelson Rockefeller. It was suggested at the time that they liked the feeling of being able to do a favor for a Rockefeller.

In the 1965 mayoralty campaign, it was conversationally "in" to aver that since New York was so badly governed—which it wasn't—there was just no question about voting for anyone but Lindsay. When Beame, the Jewish candidate, defeated Screvane, the Wagner choice as successor in the Democratic primary, Beame won substantial support as an adequately representative Jew among the middle and lower classes, but the upper-middle and top hierarchy voted for Lindsay.

The best example of Jewish mass pressure in favor of a Jewish nominee goes back to 1932. Herbert H. Lehman, Lieutenant-Governor under Franklin Roosevelt, and described by the latter as his "good right arm," was the choice of both Roosevelt and Smith for the governorship. John F. Curry, leader of Tammany Hall, had formed a coalition, with a majority of the state convention delegates in it, behind John Boyd Thatcher, Democratic Mayor of Albany, in opposition to Lehman. Smith and Roosevelt pressed, and Curry refused to budge. The cannier Brooklyn boss, John H. McCooey, Curry's principal partner in the coalition, realized there would be "moider" back home if as outstanding a Jew as Lehman was turned down, particularly when he would be the first Jewish Democratic candidate, if nominated and Governor, if elected.

So McCooey, who was absolute boss of his bailiwick, arranged for an overwhelming majority of his district leaders, Jews and non-Jews alike, to "revolt," and inform him that he could not control the great bloc of Kings County delegates. Lehman went on to win, and to dominate his party's politics in New York for thirty years thereafter.

## THE ITALIANS

The Italians who poured through the immigration gates at Ellis Island, in numbers at least equal to the Irish and the Jews, have not consistently participated in and influenced New York City politics to the same extent. One reason, at the beginning, was that fewer stayed here.

The big Italian push, in the same 1880 to 1910 period that marked the peak rush from Eastern Europe, was made up mainly of contract laborers imported to finish the still expanding American railroad network. To them, New York was just the place where they were to be met by the Italian agent who supplied dollar-a-day labor to the railroad builders. They were signed up in their first few steps on solid group, if they had not already been signed, with passage paid, before leaving sunny Southern Italy.

Even when railroad work was over, few returned to their native land. In almost every upstate New York community, there is, even today, an Italian population that owes its location there to the men who came to build the railroads, and later settled down to other occupations. Apart from a small professional class of doctors and lawyers, the bulk of those who did stay in New York City itself took pick-and-shovel jobs in the city's budding construction industry. A generation, sometimes two, elapsed before the illiterate peasant whose first advance was to bricklayer or hod-carrier, gained status in the construction industry as a capitalist. His original labor force consisted of himself, his sons and brothers.

At the beginning, he was apathetic, at least, to politics and the unfamiliar governmental system. He preferred to concentrate on work, raising a family, and living with people of his own language and background—an insularity by no means unique to the Italian immigrant, but just carried further. If pushed or jockeyed into a political preference at all, he leaned toward the Republicans, associating the party's name, in translation, with the Republican movement of Italy's national heroes and unifiers, Garibaldi and Mazzini. Tammany Hall, after impressing some Italians into citizenship, learned not to press him too hard to vote.

The first man to stir the Italian into political consciousness was La Guardia—not the La Guardia who was Mayor from 1933 to 1945, but the younger and even more fiery La Guardia running for Congress, starting in 1914. As an Ellis Island interpreter, he knew what made up New York's melting pot and he capitalized on it politically. He was multilingual and when addressing Jews, his campaigns were in Yiddish; when haranguing Poles, in Polish, etc. And when he talked to Italians, who abounded in the lower Manhattan district in which he first ran, he not only spoke their language, he appealed to their national pride.

There ought to be an Italian sitting in Congress, representing the Italians, he would scream, and any Italian in New York who had the chance to vote for him and didn't, was a dirty no good Austrian bastard that any other Italian should spit upon. In 1914 when he first ran, and in 1916, when he first won, denouncing the Austrians in Italian was both safe and sound. He not only won the Congress seat from what had been a Democratic district, but he went over to Italy as a member of the Army Air Force—a flying Congressman—to fight Italy's enemies in World War I. Since he ran as a Republican in those days, his status as a hero to the Italian community gave its previous Republican tendencies major reinforcement.

Tammany took a few unimaginative steps to neutralize the Italians as a group. It nominated and elected a handful to the Legislature and to places on the bench, but uniformly they were required to pay for the nominations in cash. This was not uncommon but the difference was that while not all the Irish and Jews paid, all the Italians did. Their identification with the Democrats thus was as customers, rather than members, of the dominant political establishment.

As a concession they sometimes were allowed to pay in installments, if they could not raise the whole price at once.

La Guardia's election as President of the Board of Aldermen in 1919, and as Mayor in 1933, made him the first of

his origin to hold a city-wide office. As Mayor, he never lost
the support of the Italian rank and file on Election Day,
though often opposed by the much smaller clique that had
achieved wealth and background position within Tammany.

The establishment of the Italians as a group that might consistently respond to political recognition came very slowly
within both major parties. In 1933 sparsely populated Richmond elected an Italian, Joseph A. Palma, Borough President
on the La Guardia ticket, and reelected him twice, even
though the borough's enrollment and voting tendencies were
heavily Democratic. He was favored by Democratic scandals,
his own good reputation, his running with La Guardia, and
the very heavy Italian concentration in the borough. The
fact that the Italians would, and could, influence an election
began to sink in. In 1938, when the Democrats nominated
Charles Poletti for Lieutenant-Governor—at Lehman's insistence for personal reasons—the Republicans stirred themselves
enough to put up Edward Corsi for United States Senator.

Again, in 1945, when the Democrats, for the first time,
nominated an Italian for city-wide office—Vincent Impellitteri for President of the Council, the Republicans countered
with Nicholas M. Pette for the same office. The bidding for
the "Italian vote" was on. Since then, any so-called balancing
of the ticket, city or state, has called for Italian representation, along with the Jews who had previously broken the
Irish monopoly.

What lay in the background of this new interest in the Italian vote was that, apart from the attachment to La Guardia,
the New York City Italian had swung slowly to the Democrats, with the advent of the New Deal, for exactly the same
economic reasons that swung the majority of poor and middle-

class voters of all races and origins. Then there was a setback, an alienation from the Democrats, rising from reaction to Franklin Roosevelt's "stab in the back" characterization of Italy's entrance into World War II when France was already crumbling before Hitler's assault. The Italian did not have to be a rooter for Mussolini to feel that his own pride was involved.

The second and third generation Italians increased in both literacy and political consciousness, and both parties competed for their support in the years that followed. The Italian community advanced to positions of political leadership in both parties, not only in New York City but in most of its suburbs. In the mid 1960's it still had a distinct tendency to vote Italian, when a countryman was running against a non-Italian, but it was also increasingly influenced by other issues, not tucked away in advance in the pocket of either party. In this, of course, it reflected the increasing independence of party labels manifested by the community as a whole.

## THE NEGROES

One of the basic political truths is that there is a relationship between the economic status of the citizen and how he casts his vote. The campaign manager, evaluating the issues available, will state flatly that "people vote their pocketbooks." Like any other rule, it has its exceptions—occasions when the economic factor influences, but does not control the vote.

In looking at the Negro relationship to politics in New York City, there do not seem to be any of the exceptions that from time to time have affected other racial groups. In other words, the Negro has voted as the poor and underprivileged, rather than on the basis of race or color. This is not at all surprising in view of an atmosphere which offered little other incentive.

The bulk of the Negroes who came to New York did so from the southern states, where the governing principle was to keep them so low economically, socially and politically that the "poor white trash" would be able to feel superior. Even when the southern Negro moved to New York, where at least his right to vote was always safe, he took a dim view of the prospects for either economic or social equality. He responded listlessly, if at all, to the few gestures made to interest him in politics. This tendency is still apparent, even though the Negro population of the city increased from less than 2 percent in 1900 to about 13 percent on the 1960 census figures.*

On a percentage basis, the biggest Negro migration to New York was during the 1920's, when cotton picking in the South began to wane as a means of livelihood. Many wandered North to find jobs—poor but better than none—in the big cities, including New York. Here they settled in already established small Negro enclaves in parts of Harlem, South Jamaica, and Atlantic Avenue in Brooklyn, the latter the nucleus for the Bedford Stuyvesant ghetto of later years.

College-educated Negroes who were doctors or lawyers, entertainers in nightclubs or the theater were here, also, in small numbers, but the average migrant found himself work-

* The Census Bureau Library lists the Negro population of New York City, rounded off by this author in even thousands, as follows:

| Year | Numbers |
|------|---------|
| 1900 | 60,000 |
| 1910 | 90,000 |
| 1920 | 152,000 |
| 1930 | 327,000 |
| 1940 | 458,000 |
| 1950 | 775,000 |
| 1960 | 1,088,000 |

ing as a mop-and-pail monitor in an office building or the subway, while his wife hired out as a domestic and many of the children skipped school to shine shoes.

The Negro who bothered to vote usually voted Republican. Identification with the Democratic party—the party of Jim Crow—made no sense. Woodrow Wilson, the last Democratic President, had a position on the Negro that was southern and archaic. When the Democrats in Tammany Hall—faced with a fast growing Harlem Negro population—started courting Negro support at the polls, they did it with the cynical, ward-heeler approach, with bait of cash, petty jobs or petty favors. The clubhouses which did get Negro members maintained segregation—the Negroes in the basement, the whites upstairs. The Harlem area was kept from being a political entity by assembly and aldermanic district lines deliberately designed for that purpose.

The first Tammany recognition of the Negro as an officeholder was tied in with the petty job concept. Ferdinand Q. Morton, who served as a Negro Tammany straw boss in Harlem, was appointed to the Municipal Civil Service Commission by Hylan in 1922 and he stayed on under Walker, O'Brien, La Guardia, and into the O'Dwyer administration, as one of a three-man board passing on Civil Service rules and administration. He never succeeded, if he ever seriously tried, in opening up the Civil Service to the Negro beyond the same messenger, cleaner, janitor jobs that private industry offered.

A turning point came with the election of Roosevelt as President and La Guardia as Mayor. Roosevelt's promises of better things for the hungry and needy turned Harlem Democratic in 1932, for the first time in a presidential election. As FDR worked hand-in-glove with La Guardia, the local Civil Service, both city and federal, were opened up. The Negro

from then on could get a job as changemaker, and later con-
ductor and motorman, in the subway system. City department and agencies began hiring Negroes as clerks, secretaries
and even technicians.

La Guardia had a technique of his own for putting pressure
on the big department store owners to break the color barrier.
A leading merchant would be invited to dine with the Mayor.
Somehow he would find that his fellow guests, all big names
in various fields, would be discussing discrimination in employment. He would be the only one out of step and before
the evening was over, made commitments, under this social
pressure, that went far beyond what he would have made if
tackled directly at his place of business. The "act" was put
on successively for employer after employer, with a high degree of success. Mrs. Roosevelt, on the scene the way the
President couldn't be, worked closely with La Guardia. Action on half a dozen fronts served to create, or enlarge, a
Negro middle class. The number of Negroes who went to
the polls also increased, and they cast their votes consistently
for Roosevelt and La Guardia as long as they ran.

Later there were actual legislative steps, like the State Fair
Employment Practices Act of 1945, the city and State Human
Rights Commissioners, the city's own pioneer Fair Housing
Practices Law, with officeholders like Dewey, Ives, Harriman,
Rockefeller and Wagner making varying contributions.

But the major things that tied the Negro to his local government were public housing and public welfare. The fine
point that both these programs are financed by a combination
of federal, state and city funds, has been ignored by those
affected, who just blessed or blamed the city.

The Negro's preoccupation with bread and butter issues
served to insulate him from the world revolution propaganda

levelled at him for decades by the American Communist party. It made a few converts of intellectuals or artists, but the tremendous amount of time, effort and money the Communists devoted to the rank and file was largely wasted.

However, the Communist allies or partners who produced results visible to the Negro in his own backyard were in a different position. The Negroes appreciated Marcantonio's congressional and extracurricular services just as much as the Puerto Ricans did later. They went so far as to elect Benjamin J. Davis, Jr., Negro Communist, to the City Council, on Marcantonio's say-so, and they likewise adopted Adam Clayton Powell, Jr., who came into politics in Harlem as a spear-carrier for Marc. Powell won the election as his mentor had done, first as a Republican, then as both a Republican and nominee of the Communist-controlled New York County American Labor party, and finally as nominee of all three parties. His support later, after Marc's demise, stemmed from other factors.

These were the Negro political hierarchy built by Marcantonio and Tammany as a joint venture; the church ministry that gave him leverage with the religious-minded among the Negroes, and finally, his nose-thumbing at the white man's political rules of behavior. The latter popularized him among those who approved of anyone Negro who could beat the white man at his own game.

Negro politicians and officeholders increased steadily in the 1940's and 1950's, as they first filled up and then overflowed Harlem and Bedford Stuyvesant, so that gerrymandering could no longer deprive them of representation on the party committees and in the Legislature and City Council.

The theoretical culmination of this came with the election, in the early 1960's, of a West Indian Negro, J. Raymond

Jones, as leader of Tammany Hall, once the stronghold of the Irish. However, it represented less the recognition of the Negro as a race than of Jones' personal mastery of the art of politics.

He and Adam Powell staged for years a political act that insiders admired and enjoyed, though the newspapers treated it with complete seriousness. Jones and Powell were privately partners. Every time there was a split of importance within the Democratic party, Powell took one side, and Jones the other. That way, the partnership could never lose.

The Wagner administration, at its very start in 1954, gave the city its first Negro Commissioner, Arthur C. Ford, to head the Department of Water Supply Gas and Electricity. It followed this breakthrough with Negro membership on the Mayor's own City Hall staff, and deputy commissionerships in other departments too numerous to list.

The same year also saw Hulan E. Jack come into the Negro's highest elective office, the Borough Presidency of Manhattan. Jack's election was triggered by a chain of events. First the Republicans broke tradition by nominating a Negro for the office. Then the Liberal party, fielding a city ticket of its own, followed suit, and so did the Democrats. Running on the Wagner ticket, Jack won easily. There was no test of what the vote would have been like if only one party nominated a Negro, and there is not likely to be such a test for a while.

Although Jack left his office before the end of his second term, under fire, his successors were Edward Dudley and Constance Baker Motley, both Negroes, establishing the tradition for the time that the Borough Presidency of Manhattan belonged to the Negro race, just as it had years earlier to the Jews.

Dudley and Mrs. Motley were extremely competent office-holders and leaders in key years when the agitation grew for complete rather than token equality of opportunity for the Negro. They were the first who campaigned and acted on the basis of improvement of the living and housing standards of the community as a whole, with the Negro as an integral part.

This was an important step forward in lifting the Negro's stake in politics above the ward level.

## THE PUERTO RICANS

The Puerto Rican migration to New York differed in its political aspects from the preceding Irish, Jewish, Italian and Negro invasions. It was the first that saw politicians in power cater to the new arrivals even though very substantial segments of the electorate already on hand disapproved. The result of this was that the newcomer from the Caribbean was absorbed faster into the political structure of the city than the other non-English speaking arrivals from Southern and Eastern Europe half a century earlier.

The political facts of life of the Puerto Rican in New York may be summed up as follows:

He, like the Negro from the southern States, was already a citizen, with normal voting rights if he chose to exercise them.

His arrival in numbers was at the same time that the movement to eliminate discrimination against the Negro was gaining new momentum, and the dark-skinned Puerto Rican, while counted in the census figures as white, benefitted from everything stirring in behalf of the Negro.

Finally, his was the first major migration to land in a social system of community responsibility for the underprivileged, so that even though the Puerto Rican was paid below scale for his labor and outrageously overcharged for the roof over his head, there was a government prepared to make up the gap between income and outgo. This led unjustly to the charge that he came here to go on relief; the truth was he came to find work.

He was resented on the one hand by the immigrants of different stock who were by then third generation Americans, but he was nevertheless welcomed by a substantial segment of the business community that needed him to fill unskilled and semiskilled jobs in trades and industry. This business support bolstered the position of the political officeholders who recognized the Puerto Rican as new voting fodder.

The first to do so was the always alert and astute Italian Vito Marcantonio, whose political bailiwick included an already established "Spanish Harlem." When the Puerto Rican migration gathered steam and headed on arrival here for the neighborhood in which Spanish was spoken, Marcantonio encouraged the newcomers to the utmost. Political opponents charged he even flew in Puerto Ricans by chartered plane in advance of elections in which he had a personal interest. There is no evidence to substantiate that, but it is true that Marcantonio, given the opportunity to cultivate new and needy immigrants the same way Tammany had done half a century before, made the most of his chance. He gave them help in finding shelter, getting a job, battling the landlord, obtaining assistance from the Welfare Department and the Health Department, furnishing legal aid, all in exchange for support at the polls.

He was able to help in a big way because at the time the migration became heavy, in 1946, and for several years thereafter, he was the undisputed political boss of Harlem, with the governmental prerogatives that go with that status. When he was finally defeated in 1950, the Puerto Rican community, which did not have time to develop political leadership from within its own membership, or establish ties with the major parties, was briefly bereft of political contact with the outside world. But this was not for long.

The Puerto Ricans still lived mostly in Manhattan, spreading from Spanish Harlem along the East River to Manhattan's West Side. Their shelter was in good old apartment houses and brownstones hastily and flimsily converted into rooming houses, with a whole family to a room. A loophole in the law, freeing these accommodations from rent control, made this type of overcrowding exceedingly profitable to a type of landlord who was dubbed "slumlord" for the conditions he created.

It was natural for Robert F. Wagner, Jr., then Borough President of Manhattan, to have the most contact with the Puerto Ricans, and a combination of social consciousness and political acumen moved him rapidly into the vacuum created by Marcantonio's political demise. At first Wagner was able to give his new Latin constituents only tokens of recognition—important to them—such as an annual message on their great fiestas, always printed in the Spanish press; an exchange of students between New York and San Juan; an operating relationship with the federal bureau in charge of Puerto Rican affairs; an always extra-warm welcome to Commonwealth dignitaries and functionaries.

Before most English-speaking politicians were aware of it, Wagner was the only major New York officeholder known to the Puerto Rican New Yorker. When the veteran Senator Wagner died in the spring of 1953, the press of New York and the nation recalled the Senator's leading roles in the halcyon days of the New Deal. New York's Spanish paper, "La Prensa," noted that Borough President Wagner's father was dead.

As Mayor, Wagner was able to do much more for the Puerto Rican than send holiday greetings. He tore into the evil of the family-in-a-room apartment, eventually abolishing it; he spurred the creation of Spanish-language auxiliary teachers in the school system to overcome language barriers for the hordes of Puerto Rican youngsters; he fought and beat recurring attempts to require a year's residence before even supplemental welfare checks could be paid out; he made sure that food items familiar to the newcomers were made available in the federal surplus food program.

The city established sound trucks—known irreverently by the City Hall staff as "Bitch Buggies"—that parked in crowded neighborhoods to receive complaints from the citizenry, and give out advice on city services available. They concentrated, quite naturally because of the need, in the Puerto Rican neighborhoods, which by the late 1950's were not limited to Manhattan, but included whole sections of Brooklyn and The Bronx. The newest migrants had every opportunity to feel that their government, their DEMOCRATIC city government—was interested in their welfare.

The result was that the Puerto Rican voters threw their lot with the Democratic party in greater percentage than any other new arrivals since the original Irish affiliation with Tammany Hall a century before. Election margins of 20 to 1 for the Democratic ticket in Puerto Rican areas became almost commonplace.

Wagner's identification with the Puerto Ricans served him well when he fought the party organizations in the 1961 primary campaign. They voted for him and his ticket right down the line. Even in the 1965 campaign, when the Democrats lost the mayorality, the party's nominee did far better in the Puerto Rican areas than elsewhere.

The 1965 election was less than two decades after the Puerto Ricans started moving here in force. They still numbered only 600,000 out of a city population of nearly 8,000,000. Yet they were able that year to elect one of their own as the Borough President of The Bronx, on the Democratic ticket. No other group achieved political recognition that fast. The political establishment with which they had to deal was a far different one than that which had confronted their predecessors, in that voting at all levels had become commonplace, and was associated far more closely with living conditions. The Puerto Rican faced discrimination in many places, but not at the polls.

# 7.   The Anatomy of Graft

In the mid-1950's a high official in the city's Wagner administration was escorting a visiting Latin American dictator
from a City Hall reception uptown to an official welcoming
luncheon. As they drove on one of the north-south avenues
that showed off the city's boom in new skyscrapers, the visitor said:

"So much construction. *You* must be doing very well."

The New Yorker started to explain, then realized that he
couldn't—without embarrassing the city's guest—that in New
York there was no longer a system of percentage collections
on construction or anything else, for the benefit of top officialdom. And no matter how delicately he put it, there was the
probability that he would not be believed. So he just joined
his visitor in admiring the view. Influence peddling exists, but
the peddler is not in partnership with the official whose "favor" is offered for sale.

It has been many years since top city government or political leaders have taken personal graft. They disapprove of
it for their underlings, and those who do "take," risk jail and

disgrace. Yet graft still exists and so does the legend that because big city governments have bred graft from time immemorial, New York, the biggest, has the biggest grafters.

Civilization and graft seem to run in parallel. Rules and regulations are laid down progressively with the encroachment of civilization, to keep one man from taking undue advantage of another. As rules increase, graft grows under foot, to pay for advantage or avoidance of penalties under the same rules and regulations. In the cities, with more rules and more wealth, graft was commonplace. In the rural areas, the country slicker sold gravel and sand to the town board of which he was a member, rigged a tax assessment, or the sale of acreage held in default of taxes, that is, he took advantage of his limited opportunities. He publicly damned his city cousin as a thief while he privately envied the latter's greater opportunities for loot. More than differing ethical standards, this is responsible for the image of the big cities as the sinks of iniquity in an otherwise politically pure America. New York, as the biggest city, has thus been projected for decades as the bellwether of the grafting flock.

Not since the turn of the twentieth century has New York's government rivalled in corruption the Chicago of Big Bill Thompson, the Boston of Jim Curley, the San Francisco of Abe Ruef, the Kansas City of Jim Pendergast, or the Philadelphia of Bill Vare and his original successors. And there are cities and villages in New York State itself where the techniques of dishonesty still flourish.

New York's symbol of graft and grafters is William Marcy (Boss) Tweed, who took control at the start of the Civil War and wasn't jailed until the end of the Reconstruction Era in 1876. Even today the cartoon of this burly bully in prison stripes, drawn originally by Thomas Nast, is used to illustrate the grafter in the history books, the weekly news magazines and the daily press. He is the most notorious of them all.

The story of graft in New York at its peak and through its decline can best be told by eras, in terms of the types of looting and those people who did it.

## Tweed and Post Tweed—1860-1898

Tweed was the leader of Tammany Hall, which dominated the ruling Democratic party, and also was the ringmaster of an inner circle of the crudest sort of thieves. The gang kept two sets of books, one to show the public the total cost of running the city, and the other for themselves to keep track of their share. In charging for a court house—the Tweed Court House in 1966 was still standing forlornly in City Hall Park—their bill-padding reached all-time heights. Each chair costing $15 was billed to the city for $300, and the same scale went for every item in construction or furnishing of the edifice.

This was an elementary type of larceny, the kind for which the Tweed gang is best remembered. It worked just so long as they owned the auditors and had the judges as partners. It was the phony books that ruined them in the end, when some of the thieves fell out. The then crusading *New York Times* obtained and printed facsimiles of the pages, the gang broke up, Tweed fled and later went to prison.

Bill-padding was not the only type of larceny they employed. They appointed the city's policemen, who thereafter worked for, or with them, in levying on the liquor and vice industries. The Tweed Board of Aldermen, the city's ruling body, sold franchises to the highest bidder among the budding gas and trolley car tycoons. Tweed himself sold judicial and legislative protection and assistance to Jim Fisk and Jay Gould, who were busy fighting to control, monopolize and rape the railroads which served the city.

In various forms more than $30,000,000 was traced to the Tweed ring, and the amount untraced was probably many times greater. The men who followed Tweed as leaders of the still-dominant Tammany Hall were "Honest" John Kelly and Richard Croker, who discarded the crudest of the Tweed tactics—milking the city treasury by bill-padding and fake records. They and their adherents continued to live off the protection of prostitutes, extortion from saloon keepers, the sale of franchises and legislation in Albany and at City Hall.

Neither Kelly nor Croker ever went to prison, but neither did anyone believe they maintained their standards of living by honest endeavor. In the days of no income tax bureau, and a public that expected politicians to be crooked, the office-holder or boss could wear his diamond stickpin, flash his bankroll, and buy drinks for the crowd without embarrassment. Hardly anyone was so crude as to question where Croker got the money to maintain racing stables here and abroad.

### CONSOLIDATION TO DEPRESSION, 1898-1930

Tammany Hall retained the political leadership of the big city which came into being through the 1898 consolidation. Though the outlying areas in Kings, Queens and Richmond contained more acres, and eventually more people, the money and power remained in Manhattan.

For twenty-two years, from 1902 to 1924, one man was leader of Tammany Hall. Charles Francis Murphy was possibly not the inventor of "honest graft," but he was its adapter to the needs of the political organization he headed. By the time of his death he was regarded as the sagest, most conservative in the field. By the standards of that day, though not this, he stood out against unbridled corruption.

History looks back on Murphy as the absolute ruler of the political province. He was not. Originally he had to fight off reformers, such as the once important Citizens Union, and grapple with the unending ambitions of William Randolph Hearst. He lived through the antics of Charles Parkhurst, crusading minister; the activities of William Travers Jerome and Charles S. Whitman, two crusading district attorneys; three Mayors, Seth Low, Gaynor and Mitchel, whom he did not control, and Hylan, whom he controlled only to the extent that Hearst permitted.

Possibly because Murphy could never be as sure as his predecessors and some of his successors, of winning the mayoralty and governorship; possibly because of innate common sense or enlightened self-interest, the Murphy era was the first in which things were ruled out because they were "too raw." Murphy never tried to eliminate police graft at the top or in the ranks, but he did clamp down on party or police protection of organized vice. Franchises were no longer sold openly. An example of the Murphy method shows up in the construction of the new and then grandiose Penn Station. The permits for the closing of streets needed for the immense railroad terminal were held up by the Murphy-controlled Board of Aldermen until the railroad gave the excavation contract to the firm in which Murphy had a financial interest. Tom Smith, Murphy's longtime associate as Secretary of Tammany Hall, set an example in moderation that won him popularity among the district leaders when he restricted his outside activities to owning the company that did all the city printing, and did not seek a cut of anything else.

Judgeships were sold for high prices to aspiring lawyers but once they had donned the judicial robes neither they nor others who reached the bench as a reward for loyal party service were expected to corrupt justice—except in the lower criminal courts where the party continued the system of police, and political protection of those who would pay for non-interference with illegal enterprises.

In Albany, the so-called "Black Horse Cavalry," which raided business by sponsoring legislation adverse to some particular trade—and then dropping the bill for a price—functioned in the early years of the Murphy period. When the group was exposed and dispersed, Murphy, whose legislators were only part of a bi-partisan troop, never rallied them for new operations.

Murphy's lasting contributions to higher political standards came from a number of other things.

He developed and pushed the careers of some men of real competence as legislators and high officeholders, whose achievements stood him and Tammany in good stead during his latter years and enhanced his reputation after he was dead.

His own son-in-law, Surrogate James A. Foley, was one of the most learned and respected men ever to sit on the New York bench. Foley was even elected to succeed Murphy as leader of Tammany Hall, but resigned the following day on the afterthought that he preferred the cloister of the bench to the rough and tumble of political leadership. Robert F. Wagner, Sr., another protégé, served as a legislator and legislative leader, went on the bench, and then to the United States Senate, where he won national fame as the legislative sponsor of the pioneer laws in the fields of labor relations, social security and housing.

Outranking all others was Alfred E. Smith. Murphy brought him up through the ranks, as a big league baseball manager would a potentially great ballplayer, all the way to the governorship, where Smith set a historic pattern of Albany statesmanship. Smith's nomination for the Presidency, which eventuated in 1928, was a Murphy project very much off the ground when Murphy died in 1924. All of the men he sponsored who reached high office were personally financially honest and Murphy never asked them to be otherwise. The lone exception was Jimmy Walker, who reached the mayoralty after Murphy died.

Both on his own, and with the help of his better officeholders, Murphy accepted the concept of social reform through governmental action, a pattern up to then unknown to city machines. The masses of immigrants to New York, mainly from Eastern Europe in his era, latched onto the Democratic party as a result, and the allegiance has not been lost since. The Democrats became, in New York, the party of the common man. Murphy's evaluation that "it brings votes" was correct.

The Murphy-era phenomena, honest men in high office, plus party social consciousness, link up with the graft story because they built the foundations for the much higher standards of governmental action and honesty that were to come in the La Guardia-Roosevelt era.

When Murphy died, he was hailed as having created a "New Tammany," but several things happened fast to worsen, temporarily, the political climate. First was the increasing feeling that the Prohibition Amendment and the Volstead Act, which made liquor selling a crime, were laws that even

The Anatomy of Graft

politicians and law enforcement officials should not take too seriously.

This author, covering in 1926 one of his first political assignments, a public political dinner, was shocked to find the Mayor, Police Commissioner, District Attorney and members of the judiciary gayly quaffing the best alcoholic beverages the local bootleggers could provide. The shock was not that they drank, but that they drank so publicly. Subsequent dinners made the experience routine, which in truth it was.

Bootlegging being a crime, it was taken over at the very start, at least at the wholesale level, by those with a criminal bent. It rapidly furnished manna for the police and the political organizations of both parties. They furnished protection at both the local and federal level in return for a share of the higher prices of beer and whisky.

In New York, the liquor mobs never quite ran the city, as Capone did Chicago. The murders of rivals over the profits of "Rum Row" were individual rather than wholesale. An otherwise moribund Republican organization was able to "take care" of the federal prohibition enforcement machinery, while the Democrats gave local police protection, also for cash.

One exception to the latter was in The Bronx, run by Murphy's selectee, Ed Flynn. Early in the game, one of the rising bootleg barons walked into Flynn's office in The Bronx, tossed an envelope containing $200,000 in big bills on Flynn's desk, and told him it was his, in return for the franchise to run beer in The Bronx.

Flynn said, in effect:

"You're already running beer in The Bronx. The people of The Bronx want beer, so keep on running it, but under two conditions. Take that dirty money out of here and don't try to give it to anyone else in The Bronx. Second, if you have any dirty work to do, do it someplace else. The first time there's a bootleg gang murder up here, you're through."

There never was a bootleg murder in The Bronx, or if there was, the body had been carted to another county before it was found. The rackets that followed repeal were not tolerated there either.

The city-wide political leadership that Tammany still enjoyed fell into the hands of men lesser in stature than either Murphy or Flynn. George W. Olvany served five years after Murphy died, to be succeeded by Curry early in 1929. Under them the individual district leaders emerged as powerful grafters without supervision or restriction; it was every man for himself. Both Olvany and Curry themselves were shown up later in the Seabury investigation as men who made money out of politics through not particularly subtle use of power.

Al Smith, who could have been the real boss, was devoting his time to seeking the presidency and Jimmy Walker was Mayor. Jimmy was the symbol of New York in the speakeasy era—easy money (easy come, easy go); nightclubs, climbing skirts, climbing stock market. He didn't give a damn about money—who gave it to him, who got it, or where it came from, as long as he or a friend had it to spread around for a good trip, a good party, a not-so-good girl. One anecdote will suffice.

On the recommendation of a Tammany district leader typical of his ilk, Jimmy appointed a certain honest though unprominent lawyer as a city magistrate. The man resigned the day after his appointment. He had not quite understood the district leader's language and was not willing to pay the $10,000 the leader had expected. Jimmy was getting no part of the money, but he promptly accepted the resignation and appointed another lawyer with a greater understanding of what the $10,000 was for.

Jobs thus were being sold and resold without the Mayor caring; the top political leadership was feathering its own nest, police graft was the easiest and safest in a decade; graft so permeated the governmental and political structures that it came to be regarded again as the normal way of life. There was no sign that the citizenry cared, either. Fiorello La Guardia ran for Mayor in 1929, basing his entire campaign on charges of Tammany graft, and Walker won by a record majority.

After the stock market crash came the depression, and the boom in graft sank lower than the Dow-Jones averages. The one difference, looking back, is that there was no such comeback in the graft market as there was over the years in Wall Street.

## THE DEPRESSION, LA GUARDIA AND ROOSEVELT, 1930-1945

As a matter of sound general public policy . . . where a public official is under inquiry or investigation, especially an elected public official, and it appears that his scale of living, or the total of his bank deposits, far exceeds the public salary which he is known to receive, he . . . owes a positive public duty to the community to give a reasonable or creditable explanation of the sources of the deposits, or the source which enables him to maintain a scale of living beyond the amount of his salary.

(*The Public Papers of Governor Franklin D. Roosevelt, May 1932.*)

Roosevelt's ruling was delivered in the proceedings for removal from office of New York County Sheriff Thomas J.

Farley, "Tin Box Tom," who was also a prominent Tammany district leader. The day it was laid down and Farley was removed from the shrievalty, it was properly viewed as aiming a pistol at the head of Mayor Walker, also under investigation. The lasting effect was even greater. It set a precedent that holds to this day so far as either elected or appointed politicians in office are concerned. Besides increasing the chances of punishing a grafter where sufficient definite proof was lacking, it provided a common meeting ground, still in use, for government tax men and local prosecutors. It paved the way for the enactment, at the state constitutional convention in 1938, of the requirement that an officeholder, called before a grand jury for questioning about his acts in office during the previous five years, must waive his constitutional immunity against self-incrimination. If he fails to do so, he forfeits the office he holds and is ineligible for another for the next five years. The Farley case, in its timing, the bottom of the depression, and its target—the hulking beetle-browed sheriff—couldn't have been better selected. The backdrop for the show was the famous Seabury investigation, which had evolved from previous scandals.

Starting in 1930 and continuing into 1931, a batch of city magistrates got into various kinds of unconnected difficulties. One was charged with wife beating. Another was present at a private dinner party at which uninvited guests robbed the assemblage of $17,000 in cash and left without anybody reporting the incident to the police. The implication was that undesirables on the police "wanted" list were among the judge's invited fellow diners. A third magistrate was indicted by a federal grand jury in a mail fraud case, leading to a check of his accounts, which in turn showed that he had paid a district leader for his appointment to the bench.

# The Anatomy of Graft

The Appellate Division of the Supreme Court, which had
—and still has—the constitutional mandate to keep the lower
courts in order, got stuffy about the situation. It ordered a
sweeping investigation of the magistrates' courts and in charge
it placed the white-haired Samuel Seabury, descendant of the
nation's first Episcopal Bishop, who himself looked like a
bishop. There was nothing impractical or unworldly about
Seabury, who in his earlier years had been active in city politics. Sixteen years previously he had even run for Governor
on the Democratic ticket, only to be knifed by Tammany.
He proved a master fact finder, developing to a fine art the
tracing of cash and the asking of nasty questions as to where
it came from. The dragnet he threw out to locate bank accounts and safe deposit boxes, in other states or in the names
of near relatives, was an innovation then, though today it is a
standard for investigators. He uncovered judge after judge
who had bought his job, or had taken money for fixing cases,
or both—corruption throughout the system. These revelations
in turn led to the extension of the court probe to a general
investigation of the whole city government. The last was
theoretically carried on by a committee of the State Legislature, but actually it was run with an iron hand by Seabury
himself.

Before things got that far, a powerful leader of the Legislature, an upstate Republican but close friend of Walker's from
their legislative days together, was afraid Jimmy might be
hurt. In a position to stop the broader inquiry before it started,
he called the Mayor.

"They'll get nothing on me," Walker assured him, and the
Legislature voted the investigation. In the two years that
followed, Tammany and its allied machines showed up alternately brazen and craven, corrupt and stupid. Some politicians

blubbered, some lied, when faced with Seabury's figures and inferences. Sheriff Farley—no relation to Jim Farley of Roosevelt ties—made the tin box the everlasting symbol of the grafting politician. He told Seabury all of the money he had came out of such a box. He was less certain how the money got into the box.

An equally unbelievable witness was Brooklyn's Jim Mc-Quade, whose story was that the money traced to him was just money he had borrowed for the support of relatives. He listed thirty-four relatives thus supported. Since McQuade was notoriously tight-fisted with his revenue from the police-protected crap games in his Greenpoint clubhouse, the headlines about the "34 starving McQuades" were less than funny to the citizenry.

During the boom years, the voters had been tolerant of grafting. They had felt an empathy with the politicians who took care of their jury notices and traffic tickets. The poor had accepted the traditional Thanksgiving and Christmas turkeys distributed from the clubhouses, the picnics and boat rides for the kids in summer, and had given their votes as requested by the district leaders. But in the depths of the depression, when people were jobless, hungry and losing their homes, it turned out that the Tammany Robin Hoods had stolen at least $100 for each $1 given as largesse, the reaction was devastating.

Even Jimmy Walker's popularity sank to an all-time low. Incredible digging by the Seabury staff had turned up an accountant, Russell Sherwood, unknown in politics, who was a co-holder with the Mayor of various safe deposit boxes, bank accounts and securities. Jimmy's explanations of gifts and loans were lame. Eventually, with the Farley case as a precedent, Walker was brought before Governor Roosevelt on re-

# The Anatomy of Graft

moval changes filed by Seabury. In September 1932, on the eve of probable removal from office, Jimmy resigned.

Ironically, Roosevelt, already the Democratic nominee for President, carried into office in the special mayoralty election held simultaneously with the presidential poll, Tammany's selection to succeed Walker. He was a ponderous Surrogate named John P. O'Brien. In the year O'Brien served, he showed himself too dull-witted even to be a good stooge. Also the city was bankrupt and Tammany had brought it there, the people felt. O'Brien never had a chance, and he was succeeded by a man who made a fetish of money-honesty.

Fiorello La Guardia served for twelve years—January 1, 1934 to December 31, 1945—a city administration in which there was no toleration of graft or grafters. It is true that he condoned the strange maneuvers of his protégé, Marcantonio, but he probably drew comfort from the fact that Marcantonio's underworld, Communist, Republican and Tammany alliances involved only political power, not graft, for Marc. The public didn't know about them, anyhow, until after Fiorello died, and his impact on the people was accepted by all succeeding administrations at least to the point of giving lip service to the La Guardia standards of money-honesty.

## CONTEMPORARY, 1945-1965

William O'Dwyer and Vincent Impellitteri, who shared the eight years in City Hall following La Guardia, gave that required lip service. Robert F. Wagner, Jr., who served the next twelve, gave much more. The gradual letdown from the La Guardia insistence on actual money-honesty in government was checked, possibly permanently.

Wagner, son of the old Senator had, when he assumed office, his father's name as his greatest public asset. He adhered, as long as he remained Mayor, to an original determination to keep the family name unsullied. It was relatively easy for him, since he was financially independent and owed no personal political allegiance to corrupt political elements.

Carmine G. De Sapio, by then Tammany leader, regarded graft by officeholders as just plain out of fashion, and he more than anyone else furnished Wagner's original political backing. Ed Flynn, to whom De Sapio sold Wagner as the best candidate to run against Impellitteri, had never believed in graft as a political way of life. Alex Rose of the Liberal party, who succeeded to the role of the Mayor's Warwick when De Sapio was thrown to the wolves of political reform, did not think in terms of financial gain, but in terms of newfound power.

As a result, in the three Wagner administrations, there was no toleration of graft from the top, nor major influence working in its behalf at any level. It is almost amazing that it continued to exist. But it did, and as of this era, the principal profitable operating fields for the grafter were:

1. Police.
2. Inspectional services.
3. Public contracts.

## POLICE GRAFT

Starting with Tweed and continuing to O'Dwyer's time, the policeman on the beat, the captain in the station house, the top brass at headquarters, were basically dependent in their careers on the politicians. For example, Lewis Valentine, later La Guardia's Police Commissioner, was broken from

Inspector down to Captain—his protected Civil Service rank —and transferred from Manhattan to rural Staten Island. His crime had been that he insisted, during the Walker administration, in raiding gambling houses from which Jimmy Hines, most powerful individual Tammany district leader, was getting protection money.

It boiled down to the fact that the policeman who looked the other way was rewarded; the one who interfered with a politically protected enterprise was punished, demoted, transferred. The chain of control went from the gambler or bootlegger to the district leader, who had the ear of the county leader, who had the ear of the Mayor, who told off the Police Commissioner. Sometimes for the sake of delicacy the Mayor was left out of it, but the Police Commissioner got his orders anyhow. George V. McLaughlin, Walker's first Police Commissioner, had been sponsored for the job by Al Smith, who counted on McLaughlin to keep graft in check. McLaughlin quit in disgust in less than a year.

In connection with the illegal enterprises that the police were ordered to allow—protected gambling, bookmaking, policy, speakeasies—a system of graft for the police themselves operated side by side with the political graft. It was governed only by the amount of squeeze an enterprise could afford.

With the advent of Wagner as Mayor there was a radical shift. The newspapers had been full of an exposé of a police-bookmaker alliance that had operated through the O'Dwyer and Impellitteri regimes. The incoming Mayor sat down with the political boss, De Sapio, and the two found themselves in complete agreement that:

1 Police scandals always tarred the administration in power, with no commensurate political gain;

2   The possibility of totally eliminating police graft was dim, but that the administration and the party could avoid being smeared by naming some outstandingly honest and competent man as Police Commissioner, and,

3   Allowing him to run his department without interference in fact by the Mayor or anyone else, except where broad public policies were involved, and,

4   That all promotions, demotions, transfers, etc., were to be considered routine Police Department business on which the Commissioner had the sole as well as final say.

This approach was used by Wagner in dealing with four separate police commissioners during twelve years in office. It had the effect of eliminating, completely, the political protection of the lawbreaker, or protection of the police who preyed on his enterprise. As both Wagner and De Sapio well knew, this did not completely eliminate police graft, but it has helped. The cop now is on notice he will be fired if caught, and jailed if the evidence is sufficient. An additional deterrent has been a court decision, handed down in the mid-1950's, that a policeman lost his pension if caught any time prior to his retirement.

Bookmakers and policy-slip operators have carried on as sources of illegitimate police income. There is little public indignation over violations of the gambling laws. The policeman who allows gamblers to operate—for a price—sees the bookmakers as much the friends of the common man as was the bootlegger of an earlier era, and just as logical a source of protection money.

A second major source of police graft is the enforcement, or rather non enforcement of the parking regulations. The individual occasional violator would probably find himself locked up if he tried to bribe a policeman to avoid a ticket, but there are several established systems of payoffs. One involves the wealthy resident of the East Side who wants his car waiting for him, at the door, when he comes down in the morning. He gives a fixed sum monthly to the doorman of the apartment house, who in turn passes a fixed sum for each car on to the friendly police of the precinct. How much is involved? This author recalls a money-hungry police sergeant with more nerve than sense who estimated the value to him of an East Side assignment at $1,000 a month, and presented this as a reason for being transferred there.

Operators of parking lots and garages are limited in the number of cars they can store. By paying off the local police, they store additional cars up and down the block, at regular rates per car. Storefront businessmen pay off for the privilege of parking in front of their own establishments. Big business establishments pay for the stopping of traffic, if necessary, for their trucks when loading or unloading. No one pays a great deal, but the cumulative take is high.

## INSPECTIONAL SERVICES

The city has always had thousands of persons employed in its inspectional services, from those who examined the plans filed for a new skyscraper to those who spotted roaches for the Health Department in the corner "greasy spoon." They are so numerous, they spread in so many directions, their activities defy top level supervision on any continuing basis. For decades, if anything went wrong with something the city was supposed to supervise by inspection, the answer of the incumbent administration always was to go out and hire more inspectors. This never cured the disease.

It merely increased the number of low or medium salaried

personnel, armed with badges of authority, who could put a businessman out of business, or make him spend a lot of money he hadn't been spending, to conform rigidly to the rules and regulations he had been breaking. The businessman hoped that the new inspectors, like the old, could be made to see reason if offered financial inducements, and an important percentage of the inspection force, large or small, has habitually agreed.

Some of the inspectional rackets have been well-organized from the start, some have grown up casually. For years the classic example involved the filing of plans for a new structure with the city's Buildings Department, which must approve the plans before the builder can really start work. The department has thousands of plans pending at any one time, and the process of approval cannot begin until the blueprints are taken out of the receiving basket into which the architect dropped them.

In the beginning, an architect, late with his drawings and hoping to make up the time by cutting down on delays ahead, pinned a $20 bill on his set of plans, hoping to attract immediate attention to them, and thus get a running start on the road to approval. Someone else did the same. Both told friends, in confidence, how smart they had been. It wasn't too long before only the plans with currency attached emerged from the basket.

Later on, at the construction site, where delays could pile up costs tremendously, a contractor would not wait to see if the construction inspector was technical or broadminded. He would just push $50 into his hand, by way of greeting.

The Buildings Department was not alone in this. The Fire and Health Departments, electrical inspectors in the Department of Water Supply, Gas and Electricity, all had their inspectors and the rules to enforce, relax, or ignore. Sometimes an inspector "took" as an individual; to others, he was part of a racket run with the necessary participation by the supervisory, but non-political, personnel.

The extent to which the top level used inspectors to protect the public treasury and their own reputations is best exemplified in a case involving the New York City Housing Authority, which uses city, state and federal funds in its operations. As the city's biggest landlord, it was the biggest purchaser of fuel oil for home heating. Preheated fuel oil fills up a tank truck with fewer actual gallons, so the Housing Authority spent $70,000 a year on inspectors' salaries just to check the temperature of the oil at the time the wholesaler measured it into the delivery truck.

Eventually, a slide rule expert in the federal government figured out that if all the fuel oil the Authority bought was heated to the highest temperature possible without igniting it, the molecular expansion would cost the Authority a maximum of only $50,000 a year.

A private landlord would have given up the inspection system without a second thought; the Housing Authority did only with considerable soul-searching. It knew that if it ever was cheated with preheated oil, and the story that it had fired the inspectors ever reached the newspapers, it would be pictured as lax, rather than vigilant, with the public's money.

Low-level inspectional scandals plagued the Wagner administration for most of its twelve years in office. The best minds worked away at possible solutions, but the only one ever found was to fire the men involved. To avoid any appearance of whitewash, the departmental trials which must precede dismissal were conducted by special trial officers furnished by the Bar Association from a list of attorneys willing to serve.

## PUBLIC CONTRACTS

It was commonplace in New York, in the Tweed era, for anyone doing business with the city to count on paying off the top men in government, in fact the payoff was figured in calculating the price of the job. It was equally common elsewhere, and notorious under the Thompson regime in Chicago, Hague in Jersey City and almost anybody in Boston.

In New York of recent times, every possible safeguard against this has been written into the law and the rules. The contractor must make a formal bid in competition with any other interested contractor; he must qualify as responsible; any waiver of public bidding required unanimous approval by the city's Board of Estimate, and the same applied to giving a contract to someone who was not the lowest bidder. If he gets the contract, he is under audit while the work is going on, after it is completed, and while he is waiting for his money. There probably has never been an agency of government whose work is audited more than the aforementioned Housing Authority. It has auditors from the city, state and federal governments who live in the Authority offices, put in their work on Authority contracts and never report for work elsewhere, year in and year out.

Yet in 1965 there was a scandal on Authority painting contracts bigger than any in the Authority's thirty-year history. The painting contractors in the ring could and did, underbid any outsiders because they knew they could bribe the union supervisors and the authority's own inspectors to look the other way while the painter with the "in" cut corners on work involving 135,000 apartments painted on a three-year cycle.

A few years earlier, the hallowed precincts of the city's Board of Education turned out to have sheltered shenanigans in its school construction division, with payoffs to inspectors and supervisory personnel. Some of the profits which warranted the payoffs came from "change orders." These are changes agreed to by the contractor's men and the agency's men, during the course of construction, affecting either the materials originally specified, or the plans originally blueprinted, on which the contractor based his bid.

If the change benefits the contractor, the city is supposed to get a credit; if it will cost more, the city is billed for an "extra." The changes are usually highly technical and the city engineers who pass on them can present them in one light or another to the top authority. Advance notice that there will be leniency on change orders can be very helpful to the contractor preparing his original bid, because he knows he won't have to do the work just that way.

Another contract procedure designed to prevent larceny frequently works to promote it. It is the detailed auditing which slows up the payments to the contractor. The experienced one figures his bid to include interest on the money he knows the city is going to owe him months after he has finished the job and moved on to another. The newcomer doesn't figure that in his cost, the delays eat up his profits, and he doesn't bid again on city work. This fosters the existence of rings of contractors who know the ropes. If there is a ring in operation, with payoffs, the monies due an outsider who had the temerity to win the bid are held up even longer than the most exacting audit would require, just to make sure that that outsider doesn't invade the ring's territory again.

The rock salt scandal of the second Wagner administration had some amusing aspects. Rock salt is used in great quantity to melt the snow on the city streets. Both the city administration, and the United States Department of Justice, through its antitrust division, had reason to believe that the great national salt suppliers, charging the city $15 per ton for rock salt, were in fact ganging up on the city.

At the same time a local contractor, not in the salt business, but well-connected in many ways, made a deal with the dictator of the Dominican Republican, Trujillo, to buy Dominican salt for resale to the city. The cost to him was so low that he was able to walk away with the rock salt contract at the extremely favorable price of $9 per ton to the city.

Some of the city's pleasure in this vanished when it turned out that some of the salt delivered was poor in quality, some of the deliveries were in short weight, and that an auditor in the office of the City Controller had taken money to overlook these essential facts. Even then, it was computed by insiders, with some amusement, that the percentage not delivered, or not usable, still raised the cost of what was delivered, and what could be used, to only $11 per ton, as against the $15 charged by the long-established and thus more respectable American salt trust. However, the clarion call of civic virtue demanded that the Dominican salt and its purveyor be ruled out for the future, and the city went back to the $15 domestic variety.

Many years ago, in the Harding administration, the Teapot Dome scandal rocked the federal government. The 1920's were full of the continuing investigation and prosecution of those involved in the sale of Navy oil reserve fields to private oil companies, in return for cash for themselves. In one principal case, the high-ranking public official involved was convicted and sent to prison for accepting a bribe from an oil company executive. In a separate prosecution stemming from the same transaction, the oil company executive, though indicted and tried, was acquitted of having given the bribe.

Under the ground rules in existence today, the chances are that the oil man would not even have been tried, but would have been given immunity from prosecution in return for testimony convicting the public official. This is questionable progress, for until the businessman bribe-giver is treated the same as the government bribe-taker, corruption in government is bound to continue.

# 8. Gunmen in Government

An alliance for mutual profit between the world of crime and the world of politics came into being in every large city of the nation with the advent of national prohibition. In New York, as elsewhere, the sinister alliance outlived repeal, lasting about thirty years. In much of that period the underworld paid the established political organizations and politicians for protection against the law. In a later period, the underworld actually took control of Tammany Hall by installing its own people on Tammany's executive committee.

From the viewpoint of assured protection, the racketeers did better when they were buying it for cash across the counter. The underworld's entrenchment inside the political machine itself brought in little but an increase in social standing.

There were gangs in New York almost from the beginning of its history. Killers were for hire long before prohibition. For example, the famous Rosenthal murder. In 1912 Police Lieutenant Charles Becker arranged for the murder of gambler Herman Rosenthal, who was squealing all over town that Becker was his partner and was double-crossing him. The men who committed the murder—Lefty Louie, Gyp the Blood; Dago Frank and Whitey Lewis—were pros whom Becker never met, just hired.

The prohibition gangs worked together for a single purpose, running and wholesaling liquor. A gunman who tempted to take an outside contract could get in trouble with his gang boss. Though at first, in fighting for position, the gangs committed intramural murders, later they divided the territory like big business corporations flouting the anti-trust laws. As a general rule each mob, through its recognized leader—an Owney Madden, or a Dutch Schultz—bought the necessary police and political protection from the political boss of the particular area. There was one exception to this system of local stewardship. It was James J. (Jimmy) Hines, who assumed the role and perquisites of overlord. Hines' own political district lay generally north of Central Park. As its political chief, he picked and gave support to some of the city's best aldermen, state legislators and members of Congress. A conspicuous example of this was Samuel I. Rosenman, who rose to counsel, to the President, and later head of the great Bar Association of the City of New York. In 1929, Rosenman was Hines' Assemblyman.

On the seamier side, Hines had helped or selected the district leaders on the whole West Side, including the Broadway area of the Gay White Way, most profitable of all for both bootlegger and protector. Hines supplied the protection and reaped the profits in return for continued support of the weaker leaders.

The husky handsome former blacksmith had a devil-may-care manner, plenty of brass and charm. In the very early 1920's, he defied Charles F. Murphy, at the height of the latter's power as leader of Tammany Hall, and ran an unsuccessful race against Murphy's choice for Borough President of Manhattan. As the ballots were still being counted on primary night, Hines' principal lieutenant was beaten up by Murphy men. In pure bravado, a group of Hines' men drove slowly past Murphy's own Gas House district clubhouse, the Anawanda Club on Second Avenue, and riddled the door with a volley of shots.

Hines' influence grew with Murphy's death three years later; he became the principal protector of the liquor and gambling concessions on the West Side, the theatrical district and in Harlem. On the East Side, local men ran their own shows and on the lower East Side a confederation known as the Ahearn crowd stuck together in protection and politics. There was less money in liquor in the other boroughs, and many local leaders avoided involvement. Whatever protection money was paid went instead through the hands of the precinct police captain.

The first break in doing business this way—with the politician on top—came in 1931. One Albert Marinelli, later County Clerk of New York County, announced his candidacy for the district leadership on the lower East Side already held by Harry Perry, a member of the Ahearn crowd, and tied in by marriage with the Sullivan clan, Tammany's oldest Irish political family. Marinelli moved in with the support of Charles (Lucky) Luciano, boss of the newly important Italian mob. Perry's public payroll post was Chief Clerk of the City Court. One day two of Luciano's men walked into Perry's office in the old Tweed Court House, 70 feet from City Hall, patted the guns in their pockets, and said:

"Perry, Lucky has a message for you. You're through."

Perry gulped and muttered an "okay."

This author, aware of the impending primary contest, but not of the visitors to Perry's office, asked Perry several days later if he planned to fight to keep his leadership.

His answer was: "Do you think I'm crazy? Do you think I want my people shot down in the streets? They can have it."

The incident was exceptional. Further gunpoint removals of incumbent leaders by the underworld, for replacement by their own people, waited another decade. Prohibition, when it drew to a close, released the mob manpower for ventures in full-scale racketeering, and they could not afford experimentation with the established system of protection. For the rackets, as distinct from liquor-purveying, they needed more than protection from the law in a given area; they needed help from within the offices of the countywide prosecutors, the District Attorneys of New York and Kings Counties. There wasn't too much business for them in Queens or Richmond, and they couldn't buy their way into The Bronx.

The staffs of the New York and Kings District Attorneys were so large that every district leader could and did name at least one Assistant Prosecutor. Some sponsored men who would fix a case at the drop of a word from the racketeer, provided it was forwarded with the blessing of the district leader. The final requirement was that no one at the top level in the office watch too closely or ask too many questions.

The Curry leadership of Tammany Hall guaranteed non-interference by picking, in 1929, a respectable but decrepit former judge, Thomas C. T. Crain and electing him District Attorney of New York County in the Walker mayoralty landslide that year. Crain, well over seventy, acted older. He had a mind that was clear only for the early part of the day. The fixers on the staff wore him out with needless routine in the morning, and obtained his signature or approval in the afternoon on things he was too weary to read or understand.

As a result, Crain came within a hairbreadth of removal for nonfeasance in office during one phase of the Seabury investigation, but finished his term because Seabury could not quite bring himself to recommend the removal of a fellow vestryman. What followed was worse than Crain's regime. For Crain's successor, Tammany, in 1933, picked William C. Dodge. Dodge, a magistrate, was actually the private choice of Jimmy Hines, the man he was most interested in who ran the District Attorney's office. On Election Day, La Guardia won the mayoralty for the first time by a wide margin, but Tammany managed to elect Hines' man as District Attorney. It was done by having Luciano's mobsters take over the polling places south of Fourteenth Street, where fewer protesters were likely to be. Under orders, the cops just looked the other way while the gunmen rang up votes on the voting machines as if they were fares on an old trolley car. Accomplices took over the registry books and wrote in the names of legitimate voters. Enough votes were stolen to enable Dodge to win by 11,000, out of more than 500,000 votes cast.

The victory in the long run was pyrrhic even though for the following two years the racketeers ran wild. The corner vegetable dealer who didn't pay weekly protection had kerosene poured on his produce. If he went downtown to the District Attorney's office to complain, he would find on his return home that the racketeer had been tipped off by phone and was sitting on his doorstep with an increased scale of tribute, imposed because the businessman had had the nerve to squawk.

There was so much obvious racketeering and so little evidence presented to grand juries that one of these investigating bodies decided something was fishy in the prosecutor's office. It barred the District Attorney from its sessions and composed a demand to the Governor for the appointment of a special rackets Prosecutor with his own staff.

The Governor's reaction demonstrated how New York differed from many other states. It never had a governor who truckled to the racketeers or the politicians who protected them. So the man in Albany—whether Smith, or Roosevelt, or Lehman—thus stood in the path of the total fix.

Lehman responded by appointing a special prosecutor sponsored by the Bar Association, the thirty-three-year-old Tom Dewey. He worried only because possibly Dewey was too young. Dewey was not only young, he was able, ambitious, publicity-wise, imaginative and cold as an icicle. In two years as special prosecutor, and four as District Attorney with over-all powers, he convicted and jailed Hines and Luciano; he developed an infiltration-proof system of protecting witnesses with complaints about the rackets; he wiped out the ability of the politician to furnish protection. He used for his work no one but handpicked aides and specially selected police details furnished him by Mayor La Guardia.

The underworld infiltration of Brooklyn featured the same system of alliance of underworld big shots with the district leaders, which reached into the staffs of the District Attorney, though neither then nor later, were the racketeers in control on a countywide basis.

There was enough scandal, however, to cause Governor Lehman to supersede District Attorney William F. X. Geoghan. Charges against Geoghan for laxity, dismissed after hearings, followed a sensational attempted cover-up in the Drukman murder case—a racket affair. William O'Dwyer, elected to succeed Geoghan, later won fame as the man who rounded up and convicted a gang dubbed by the newspapers "Murder, Inc."

Altogether the fanfare in the press from 1936 to 1941 made it dangerous for the politicians in Brooklyn to protect the racketeers if they got into trouble. This, on top of the New York and Bronx situations, gave the underworld slender pickings for the time.

This did not bother the central mob, Luciano's old crowd, as much as might have been expected. Frank Costello, later to become the most publicized of all the underworld figures with the exception of Chicago's Capone, had succeeded to Luciano's position as chieftain. His specialty was leasing and collecting from slot machines.

Mayor La Guardia had seized on the slot machine as the symbol of the gambling evil that helped to support the underworld. The Little Flower posed for pictures swinging an axe on piles of machines the police had rounded up by his orders. So Costello slowly switched to more legitimate enterprises, such as running his slot-machine kingdom out of New Orleans, by arrangement with Huey Long's successors, and distributing Scotch whisky, which was no longer against the law.

Some of the mobsters shifted to easy pickings in the labor union field, joining older, established syndicates brought originally into the garment trades to drive the Communists out. There was also the waterfront, a different world in which specialized mobs controlled and committed mayhem and murder almost at will, without any special political protection.

The underworld remained a political factor mostly in Harlem, where the police looked the other way if Vito Marcantonio told them to. In the areas where the racketeers continued to back, with polling-place manpower on primary and election days, the friendly politicians who had protected them but no longer could, the mobsters grew restive. This mood erupted into revolution in 1941, when they foresaw more reform even before Election Day, with no hope for return to the good old days.

La Guardia was due to be reelected for a third term as Mayor. Even worse, though Tom Dewey was leaving the New York County District Attorney's office, they were not even going to have a fighting chance of recapturing it. The events leading up to what they viewed as tragedy were as follows:

Christy Sullivan, a dull-witted relic who was leader of Tammany Hall, got the idea that the Democrats could elect a mayor in 1941 if Tammany endorsed Tom Dewey for reelection as District Attorney. Thus it would appear that Tammany was honestly opposed to sin. The offer was made to Dewey by private emissaries. He declined to run again, with or without the Tammany endorsement. He had his eye on the governorship and the presidency.

Tammany then offered to nominate any one of Dewey's assistants whom Dewey would sponsor, and Dewey sent back the names of three, all Republicans. The Tammany chieftain made a final plea—didn't Mr. Dewey have an assistant he trusted who was also an enrolled Democrat? Dewey conceded the point and proposed Frank S. Hogan, who thereafter was elected and reelected ad infinitum with the support of both major parties. Racket control of the prosecutor's office died. The underworld, even before Hogan's election, took a dim view of Sullivan's strategy. As far as it was concerned, the politicians had thrown the ball game, so the syndicate moved into the arena, putting its own men in the field. Using the manpower it had previously supplied to support district leaders, it forced resignations in the leaders' ranks. It filled those vacancies and others which occurred naturally, with its own men. Costello's gunmen actually policed the meetings at which cooperative or else frightened captains elected Costello's henchmen as district leaders and therefore members of the Tammany executive committee.

Within a year the underworld representatives constituted the largest bloc in Tammany's governing board. Costello, with the money flowing into his pockets from his gambling and slot machine empires elsewhere, was content for the most part to play the role of political patron. In 1942 Mike Kennedy was one of several candidates to succeed Sullivan as leader, though Kennedy had no support but his own single vote. Adopted as a protégé by Costello, he had a majority overnight. Costello dabbled again the following year, in behalf of a worthy Italian magistrate who deserved promotion to the Supreme Court. The magistrate, Thomas Aurelio, was duly nominated and elected, despite a last minute storm of protests, because the two major parties had divided up the judicial posts in advance, with each party supporting the other's choices.

The gale of newspaper and Bar Association protests came because District Attorney Hogan had a continuing tap on Costello's telephone, and he made public the day after the judicial conventions the transcript of a conversation in which Magistrate Aurelio pledged Costello undying gratitude for the assured promotion. The incident reflected Costello's power far more than any sinister desire to control the court of purely civil jurisdiction on which Aurelio would be sitting, for racketeers don't sue. Aurelio served out his full term with credit as an able, honest judge.

Costello could show his power when irritated, too. Mike

Kennedy, the Tammany leader he installed in 1942, he booted out right after election in 1943 because Kennedy ran away publicly from the Aurelio selection. In another case that same year, a Tammany district leader who publicly protested against the underworld influence was beaten in a primary in which Costello financed the opponent, even though the latter was an announced reformer. For the decade that followed, Tammany Hall was ruled by the underworld with never more than token dispute of its authority.

William O'Dwyer, as Mayor from 1945 through most of 1950, publicly railed against the underworld political control, but privately worked with it, or through it. For example, when O'Dwyer demanded and obtained the resignation of Edward V. Loughlin as Tammany chief—a clean-up-Tammany step taken early in the O'Dwyer administration—the word that Loughlin must go was carried to Costello, who would supply the removal votes, by Joe Adonis and Jim Moran. Adonis was one of O'Dwyer's connections with the Brooklyn underworld. Moran, O'Dwyer's closest associate, was later to be jailed for grafting.

Every Tammany Hall leader, from Mike Kennedy in 1942 to and including Carmine G. De Sapio in 1949, was selected by or with the aid and approval of Costello. By the time the De Sapio choice was made, Costello, in constant trouble with the federal government over taxes, and subject to the ministrations of an analyst, was most concerned with achieving respectability.

There are reasons to believe that when he told De Sapio the latter was to be the new leader, he also told that young man in effect:

"The Italians in politics have been smeared by some of the things of the past. Show how smart and respectable a young

Italian like you can be. Run a good, clean show, and if anyone gets out of line, let me know."

Meanwhile, a rival for Costello's underworld and political
power had emerged in the person of Thomas Luchese, also
known as Three Fingers Brown, to be identified many years
later as one of the secret rulers of the Mafia, or Cosa Nostra.
The first sign of Luchese's importance was a covert one. It
occurred in 1945, when the ticket O'Dwyer was to run
on for Mayor was announced. Marcantonio telephoned
O'Dwyer, from Washington, that O'Dwyer would have to
rearrange the slate to make room for a comparative unknown,
Vincent Impellitteri, as nominee for President of the City
Council, next in line to the mayoralty. O'Dwyer did as he was
asked, publicly giving reasons that made no sense. Some time
later Marcantonio's part in this was whispered about, and
years after, that Marc had acted at Luchese's instance.

In 1950, when O'Dwyer resigned as Mayor, and Impellitteri inherited interim title to City Hall, a special election was
held. The Costello wing of Tammany, as well as the Liberal
party, supported Ferdinand Pecora, the regular Democratic
nominee. Edward Corsi, the Republican choice, attacked
Impellitteri in the campaign as the creature of Luchese. Impellitteri, who ran independently on the No Deal ticket and
won, had the support of the Luchese bloc in Tammany, the
favoring factor that he was the Catholic of the three Italian
candidates, and the tacit approval of Tom Dewey, who as
Republican Governor enjoyed trouble for the Democrats.

This author was sitting in the office of the New York
County Republican Chairman, Tom Curran, when a call
came in from a very prominent Republican in Dewey's
statewide machine. The caller voiced the request that Curran
tell Corsi, his candidate, to "stop kicking Luchese around;

he's a client of mine." Curran curtly declined, hung up and explained the nature of the message to me.

Although De Sapio had rejected Impellitteri as a possible Democratic nominee for Mayor, and Impellitteri won, De Sapio managed to hold his leadership of Tammany Hall during Impy's three-year term. He retained the post for a variety of reasons: Costello's men remained loyal, De Sapio himself had both charm and ability, and Impy's principal aides preferred to handle the mayoralty patronage themselves, outside of party channels, rather than ferry it through a leader of Tammany Hall they might install.

Ironically, the Kefauver Senate Committee investigating and publicizing crime and rackets nationally, picked Costello rather than Luchese as the symbol of villainy at its hearings here in 1951. Luchese would have been a more timely target. When 15 Tammany district leaders, under oath before the committee, admitted under oath that they "knew" Frank Costello, the committee-fostered inference was that they still owed him fealty. A large percentage of them no longer did.

The Luchese influence figured again in the 1953 mayoralty election, when Impy was up for reelection. It was clear from the start that there would be a primary fight, with Ed Flynn of The Bronx and the De Sapio wing of Tammany backing someone to oppose the Mayor.

Impy, with an unimpressive record, and the public disillusioned about his independence, nevertheless had the backing normally accorded an incumbent by the Queens and Richmond organizations, as well as the Luchese faction in Tammany. In that situation, Brooklyn's support seemed possibly decisive. Kenneth F. Sutherland, the Brooklyn leader, was privately sympathetic to lining up with Flynn and De Sapio. When the chips were down in midsummer, he supported

Impellitteri. The word was passed that Sutherland, who knew his underworld, had yielded to pressure from Luchese.

The primary fight turned out to be a landmark in the city's politics. Wagner, the De Sapio-Flynn selection, had widespread support among social workers, parent-teacher groups, and organized labor, the latter on the strength of his father's name. He also had the better of the issues, for both recent rent and subway fare increases could be blamed upon Impellitteri's administration.

Impellitteri had the advantage which accrues in a primary to the incumbent, with support from city employees, organization-minded party workers, and an appeal to the more clannish among the Italians.

Beneath the surface, and never emerging as a campaign issue, was the fact that within Tammany Hall the issue was not Wagner versus Impellitteri, it was Costello versus Luchese. The Costello bloc was standing firmly behind De Sapio's political reform moves, and the Luchese wing fought them privately and bitterly.

When the votes in the primary had been counted, Wagner's sweep, which carried all boroughs except Richmond, eliminated, district by district, a whole basketful of leaders who stood for racket control of the political machinery.

Still others, including most of the original Costello men, became the victims over the years of the De Sapio-installed system of direct election of district leaders by the party's voters, rather than by the election district captains. De Sapio himself was eventually defeated in the same way, a victim of his own political prescience.

By the election of 1965, the underworld control of, or alliance with the political machinery, born in the days of bootlegging, had virtually disappeared.

# 9.  Cash and Candidates

The most money ever spent in behalf of a purely municipal candidate in New York City was in 1917 in the vain attempt to reelect John Purroy Mitchel as the city's fusion Mayor. The young and dashing Mitchel—the Lindsay of his day— had the moral and financial support of all of the very best people in town. They poured more than $2,000,000 into the effort, a sum never approached since. In terms of more recent campaigns, it was the equivalent of at least $6,000,000, after allowing for the difference in the value of the dollar and the fact that neither radio nor television existed then as expensive electioneering devices.

On the other hand, there were far fewer volunteer workers. Most of the Mitchel money was directed into the individual assembly and election districts theoretically for the hiring of workers, but actually for the buying and influencing of votes. The pure-minded Mitchel supporters justified this on the familiar ground of the means being less important than the end in view.

Nearly $500,000—almost a quarter of the total—was put out to foment a "revolt" in Tammany Hall. A group of Tammany district leaders were offered the money to ditch the Democratic nominee, John F. Hylan, and furnish undercover support to the Mitchel ticket. On the advice of Tammany leader Murphy, the district leaders accepted the bribes, promised support and never delivered it. The civic-minded Mitchel innocents, who thought so little of professional politicians that they assumed money could buy anyone or anything, discovered on Election Day how unethical the pros really could be, when given carte blanche.

Several object lessons seem apparent:

One is that the reformer in politics can get away with tactics that would land the professional in the hoosegow. A second is that while money is very useful in politics, there are circumstances under which money alone can not guarantee results. A third is that the amount of money spent by, or for, a political aspirant can be less important than how wisely it is spent.

A classic example of judicious spending involved Jesse I. Straus, at the time a principal owner of Macy's department store. In 1932 Straus, a firm believer in the rising star of Franklin D. Roosevelt, accepted the chairmanship of a group called the Business and Professional Men's Committee for Roosevelt for President. He knew his principal function would be to make a substantial cash contribution, and he was prepared for that. He not only believed in Roosevelt as the best man for the presidency, but he had a quiet longing for a place in the Roosevelt administration when, and if, it ever took office. His only problem was that he had no previous experience as a contributor. He laid it at the door of James A. Hagerty, the sage political reporter for *The New York Times*.

Hagerty, told by Straus that he had in mind a contribution of $15,000, advised him as follows:

> That is a substantial contribution. Don't give it all at once. Give $5,000 at the start and indicate they can come back for more if they need it. Half-way through the campaign, they'll be back. This time give them another $5,000, and indicate that that is all you intend to contribute.
>
> About a week before election, they will be so desperate for money that someone will suggest that maybe you can be induced to come to the rescue. They'll hesitate to put the bite on again, but they will, reluctantly. That's the time to give them the last $5,000. They will be very grateful, much more so than if you gave it all at once, and they spent it early.

Straus followed Hagerty's advice and events worked out as the political seer had predicted. For years thereafter, Jesse I. Straus served with distinction as American Ambassador to France, the post he wanted.

On the other side of the coin was Nathan Straus, Jr., a member of the same family, also wealthy, and perennially ambitious politically. He wanted desperately to be Governor of New York, but was willing to settle for less en route. He made substantial cash contributions to the Democratic party over a period of at least three decades. In his youth he got as high as the State Senate, serving three terms; in his middle age he was given an administrative post in housing by the Roosevelt federal administration, and in his late years, the chairmanship of a non-functioning catch-all advisory committee in the Wagner city administration. He never managed to be the right man in the right place at the right time, and no amount of money would have changed the situation.

The Republican, Nelson Rockefeller, was far luckier. He moved in on the New York State Republicans in 1958 when the GOP had no obvious, outstanding man with a claim on the gubernatorial nomination. There were, however, six contenders, all with some records of public and party service. When Rockefeller swung into action, the money power of the banks under Rockefeller control or influence cut down whatever support any of the six had. One by one they withdrew, some discreetly, some bitterly. By the time the Republican state convention was held, Rockefeller, the only candidate in the field, was nominated unanimously, and he won in a walk in the election. But his luck ran out when he sought the Republican presidential nomination in 1960 against Richard Nixon.

Rockefeller emissaries toured the country, sat down with big businessmen and big political leaders, and garnered not a single delegate. In a peculiar demonstration of political psychology, the leaders they wooed, wealthy enough to be able to resist Rockefeller pressure, were resentful of what they viewed as a last-minute attempt to have money-pressure dictate the presidential nomination.

In 1966, unlimited Rockefeller spending, possibly as much as $10,000,000, helped tremendously in lifting the Governor's third term candidacy to success—after early indications that his chances were slender. But even here, it took unthinkable Democratic stupidity to bring the GOP home safely. Rockefeller's money alone wouldn't have done it.

Fear had been expressed from time to time that the cost of campaigns has increased so much that only rich men can afford to run for public office. The Kennedys, the Rockefellers and the Harrimans are pointed out as the new types of candidates who have replaced those of the old days when it was mandatory to have been born in a log cabin.

Actually millionaires run for office now because they can get elected, whereas once their very wealth would have defeated them. The millionaire who seeks office today is not handicapped by owning coal mines where strikers have been killed, or workers exploited. Those handicaps belonged to his grandfather. The grandson's name is widely advertised to the voting public for his philanthropy and interest in the public welfare, often genuine.

Anyone of modest means can raise the money to run for office if he possesses either of two things:

A definite appeal to a particular segment of the community, or—A widespread belief that he can win.

In either case, there will be hundreds of people who will contribute, either as a matter of principle, or for the hope of personal benefit.

A labor union that contributes $25,000 offsets the contributions of five millionaires giving $5,000 apiece to the opposition and means far more in votes bound into the cause by the very act of contributing.

The first campaign of Robert F. Wagner for Mayor, waged in 1953, started off with no cash on hand for the first step, the primary battle against the incumbent Mayor Impellitteri. An effective subway car card was devised and ordered before it was discovered that $3,500, or half of the total cost, had to be laid on the barrelhead the following day. The bill was met and the crisis resolved, only by scraping the treasury of the $500 in it and getting $2,000 from Averell Harriman and $1,000 from Herbert H. Lehman in response to telephone SOS messages.

The treasury was lean throughout, with only $65,000 in contributions passing through the Wagner headquarters and an additional $65,000 in cash going to the task of "manning the polls." The latter meant about $15 for each of 4,500 election districts on primary day, for coffee, cake and carfare for the poll watchers. Both the headquarters cash and the poll expenditure totals were abnormally low, and the operation was successful only because of an unusual number of unpaid volunteers. Of course, after Wagner won the Democratic nomination in the primary and was virtually assured of election success, the money rolled in.

The need for folding money to be spent at the polls is the reason usually given for cash contributions, which are never recorded anywhere except in the memory of the candidate, his manager, and those who give. However, these surreptitious donations far exceed the amount spent at the polls, for a variety of reasons. Sometimes the donor feels that the candidate or his manager would prefer cash to a check; sometimes the donor, who wants the candidate or his manager to know that he had given, is equally desirous that no one else knows, for fear of recriminations from friends on the other side of the political fence.

Sometimes there is a third possible reason. The donor may intend to ask favors of the candidate if successful.

A gift by check is entered on the campaign treasurer's books and eventually will be reported in the public financial statement required by law. Thus, if the donor appears later as a favor-seeker, both he and the administration can be put on the spot by the newspapers. Most of what goes on in financing a campaign is in violation of some provision of some law. However, that seldom bothers anyone, for everyone including the enforcement official, is aware that these laws are silly and unenforceable. They represent pious hopes in statutory language, rather than common sense.

The most widely known of these statutes intended to govern campaign contributions is the Hatch Act, passed by Congress in 1939 which limits contributions to those seeking Federal office only. The law sets a ceiling of $5,000 on the amount any one person may donate, and a maximum of

$3,000,000 to be spent on the election of a President of the United States. Its sole effect has been to produce a system of evasions and detours worked out even before the first campaign under it has been waged. The provisions are evaded as follows:

A member, let us say, of the du Pont family wants to contribute $100,000 to elect a Wendell L. Willkie or a Dwight D. Eisenhower to the presidency. He, his wife, and three children each donate $5,000 to the Republican National Committee, for a total of $25,000. They then make similar donations to three state campaign committees, operating theoretically within state boundaries, but actually assuming other expenditures assigned to them by the party's central command. At this stage, the donor involved has contributed $100,000 completely legal, though the law limits him to $5,000.

Then the spending evasion begins. The $3,000,000 limit applies only to the outlay of a single committee. Let us say that the actual budget for the national election was $18,000,-000. The national committee of either party merely assigns sections of its spending budget to state committees. In this way six committees working toward the same end spend the $18,000,000, again perfectly legal.

The same type of restriction exists, in varying detail, at the state and city levels, putting the whole subject of limits in the never-never land. Even if a campaign treasurer slips and somehow manages to violate the law instead of circumventing it, there are no clear-cut penalties for his having done so.

Again, under the various laws passed in the field, neither corporations nor labor unions may legally make political contributions, but they find ways of doing it. The labor union may buy and donate TV or radio time that the treasurer of the campaign would normally pay for; the corporation has its executives buy tables at a fund-raising dinner and recompensates them under the table, or the corporation itself buys advertising space in a campaign "journal."

The most sensible solution would be to require a single report by a candidate or his manager that would include everything received and spent in his behalf. This would operate to reduce or eliminate the proliferation of campaign committees and family contributions. The public would then know, at least, the extent to which the candidate and his supporters had tried to buy their way in, and the measure of their success. This was the intent of the existing laws, but under them the figures that reach constituted authority are as much to be relied upon as the prospectus of a get-rich-quick oil drilling outfit.

Strangely enough the tremendous increase in campaign costs and expenditures has not produced a proportionate increase in the size of individual contributions. For the ordinary campaign, anyone who gives $1,000 is still regarded as a dear friend. The campaign schedule of many a candidate has been tailored so that the great man could spend some of his precious time at headquarters, personally thanking the $1,000 givers. The giver of $500 usually settles for a personal chat with the campaign manager, but he expects to be equally remembered after victory, and he always is, at least to the extent of receiving an audience for the request he has in mind.

Not every campaign donation that is offered or is *known* to be available is accepted or sought. Smart candidates and managers turn down donations if they feel they might be embarrassed later on the public reputation of the would-be giver.

In the Wagner 1953 campaign, an eager beaver at headquarters suggested that "if you turn me loose, I can get $5,000 from ......" The manager, to whom the name rang a faint bell, said:

"Before you tackle anybody, you should know we aren't promising anything."

Six months later the business establishment of the proposed donor was raided by the police, and the manager was duly grateful for his guess.

Others in office have suffered as the result of more subtle approaches by people who wanted an "in." A classic example involved Sherman Adams who functioned as chief of Staff for Dwight D. Eisenhower in the White House. Adams had set up and enforced rigid standards of ethics for the administration. At the same time, convinced of his own rectitude, he was naïve enough to let Bernard Goldfine, a Boston financial operator, become his "friend." Goldfine hovered close by, to take the Adams' to dinner with himself and his wife. The families exchanged Christmas presents, but on a scale that reflected the difference in their wealth, and Goldfine generally picked up the tab for a trip, on the ground that he could afford it, without ever asking a favor in return. Eventually, when the relationship was cemented, he did. It was merely, he said, for information about the status of cases in which he was involved with regulatory agencies of the federal government.

Adams used questionable judgment in forwarding the requests as his own from his White House desk. The agencies not unnaturally regarded the calls from Adams as White House intercessions, as Goldfine had undoubtedly hoped they would. When the matter came to light, Adams' position became untenable and he resigned. Had the agencies cooperated and Adams' calls never been disclosed, Goldfine would have netted an excellent return on the petty cash he had invested.

## Cash and Candidates

In New York, Sidney Ungar, Manhattan real estate operator, insinuated himself similarly into the good graces of Hulan E. Jack, Manhattan Borough President. Ungar sweet-talked Jack into remodelling, at Ungar's expense, Jack's Harlem apartment, at a time when Jack was pushing Ungar's application to be the sponsor of a city-aided housing project. Had the deal gone through without exposure, Ungar would have had a handsome return on the money he spent on the courtship. Instead, when the chain of events was exposed in the newspapers, Jack lost his Borough Presidency.

Tactics used to induce contributions from businessmen have also been known to backfire. In the 1961 mayoralty campaign, Abe Lindenbaum, an attorney who represented a number of Brooklyn builders in his private law practice, took on the task of raising funds for the Wagner campaign.

With pledges secured in advance from most of the big builders, Lindenbaum staged, at a public luncheon, the ceremony once in standard use at charity fund-raising functions. The stunt calls for the donor to rise and make his pledge publicly, as if he had just decided on it. This has the double aim of insuring recognition of the act of generosity, and possibly encouraging others to make or increase contributions. Unfortunately, in this case:

(a) The donors did business with the city.
(b) The attorney himself was a member of the City Planning Commission, which passed on projects.
(c) It was staged in the Mayor's presence.
(d) Lindenbaum had invited the press.

When the news stories were printed and a conflict of interest issue was raised, the Mayor ran rapidly away from the contributions, but accepted Lindenbaum's resignation from the Planning Commission en route.

Most city contracts are governed by provisions for public competitive bidding, and therefore there is not too much, legally, that can be done to steer city business to a friendly campaign contributor. However, the services of architects, attorneys and insurance brokers cannot be hired by competitive bidding, for the cheapest attorney, architect or broker might not be the best. As a result, they are fair game for campaign fund solicitation, and they invariably respond, with the knowledge that, all other things being equal, those who contribute will be preferred to those who don't.

Very large contributions have been made over many decades by or in behalf of individual lawyers who wanted to be judges. Many cases involved what can best be described as a straight purchase of the judicial seat and robes by means of cash given to the political leaders who could guarantee the appointment or nomination and election of the aspirant. Such transactions have generally been well identified, but seldom exposed, although they run counter to law and the accepted canons of judicial and legal ethics. There have been other transactions in the field that merely have skirted the bounds of proper conduct, contrary to what some think. These actions have not consistently lowered the standards of judicial competence, which are relatively high in the city. At least three judges whose families made very large and widely known contributions to the party coffers rose later to distinction on high counts through their own talents, though their original selections had been coincident with the cash transactions.

Needless to say, there was no year and no county in which every judge paid for his seat. Many nominations went in recognition of party service in the Legislature or in Congress.

The chairman of the law committee of the home county organization, after putting in some years as the party workhorse in election cases, could normally count on promotion to the bench. There were other lawyers who became judges because the politics of the moment called for a nonpolitical appointment or nomination.

But those who paid, paid well. In the late 1920's and early 1930's, a state Supreme Court Justice, serving on the highest court of original rather than appellate jurisdiction, received $22,500 a year in salary, for a fourteen-year term. If he paid to get on that court, the price was $100,000. In Murphy's time as leader of Tammany, this money went surreptitiously to Murphy himself, who spent it for The Hall, or kept it, as cirmcunstances demanded. In later years it was shared by district leaders important enough to claim it as political loot. When the federal income tax was finally applied to local governmental salaries, the cost of judicial nominations was lowered to $70,000, since the judge's take-home pay had been diminished.

During the De Sapio regime in Tammany Hall, the outright sale of judicial nominations was ended. Instead, the aspirant was requested to contribute a year's salary—which varied with the importance of the court—to the party organization itself to pay "campaign expenses." The aspirant also had to be politically eligible, and to be rated as qualified by his local bar association. Judges who were promoted from lower to higher courts were similarly subject to a request for a contribution. In fact, the system of promotion of judges from lower to higher courts received its greatest impetus during this era, without the organization's treasury suffering.

The sales of judgeships over the decades were limited principally to Tammany Hall men in Manhattan, and on occasion in Brooklyn, where the awarding of judicial nominations for cash or for political service depended on the standards of the Democratic boss in power. Flynn did not approve in The Bronx, reserving the posts for party and public servants without regard to cash. The Republicans in all boroughs, and the Democrats in Queens and Richmond, were seldom able to guarantee election, so that they had no consistent pattern of sale or nonsale of judicial nominations.

The recognized traffic in judgeships that did exist is the reason bar association leaders argued for years for an entirely appointive judiciary, on the theory that mayors, governors and presidents who had the appointive powers would be less likely to be influenced by cash than county or state political leaders. They overlooked the fact that the political leader powerful enough to be able to guarantee election of a judge is usually also powerful enough to secure his appointment from the Mayor, Governor or President.

Also, in plain truth, the record showed that whereas some appointive judges who paid cash for their appointments later got into trouble, there is no case on record where an elected judge, who paid for his original nomination, became involved in a scandal.

There is the story, probably apocryphal, of the political leader who sought out a judge whose election he had arranged, and attempted to influence the judge's decision in a pending case, to put in "a fix." When the judge balked at committing such an act, the leader said: "You owe this to me and the party."

"The hell I do," retorted the judge. "I paid cash on the barrelhead and don't owe anybody anything."

# 10. Life with Moses

The Biblical Moses led the Israelites through the desert for forty years. They, though not he, eventually entered the Promised Land. New York's Moses harried the people and their elected officials toward the same objective for almost as many years. Neither they nor he ever came within sight of the goal, but they covered a lot of territory en route and some of their accomplishments and experiences were memorable.

Robert Moses was born in New Haven in 1888 of mixed German and Spanish Jewish parentage, but he never practiced his parents' religion or any other. Assumedly his disdain for forms and conventions, so frequently demonstrated in his public life, extended also to those of worship. This hindered him the one and only time he sought elected office, but otherwise was unimportant. The important thing in his background was that his parents were wealthy enough to subsidize him for the career he wanted in government. He was able, even in his college days, to dedicate himself to any public service opportunity at hand without having to worry about the rent money or the possible loss of his job. As a result, it was decades before he ever lost one.

No story of the government and politics of New York City would be complete without a chapter attempting to explain the Moses phenomenon. He was both a person and an octopus in government. He ran an empire of agencies and activities without ever getting elected to public office, under the noses of those who did. He had his finger in the building of more bridges, tunnels, highways, parkways, parks and playgrounds, recreation centers, and public as well as private housing than anyone else in the city's history. Much of what he did was in the face of opposition or criticism which he ignored, overrode or compromised. In his battles, Moses had a number of things in his favor.

Personally he was handsome, vigorous, charming and gracious unless in a fight, with a fast clear mind and a fine sense of humor. He never exhibited the latter better than when he ran hopelessly and haplessly as the Republican old guard candidate for Governor in 1934, against an incumbent Herbert Lehman in a Democratic landslide year. Addressing his final rally of the campaign at Madison Square Garden, the Saturday night before election, he opened his speech as follows:

"When I started out in this campaign, I knew it was like trying to swim up Niagara Falls. Nothing has changed my mind since."

He lost by 808,000 the following Tuesday, and the Democrats even captured the Legislature. Despite that defeat— worst up to then in the state's political history—he had a hold on the imagination of the people which lasted for most of his career. It stemmed from the public's tendency to dislike red tape and politics in government. Any man who seems to fight them is likely to warm the hearts of the citizenry, and Moses made a career of denouncing both.

He also had a fine sense of public relations, keeping reporters, editors, editorial writers and publishers in his corner through his willingness to keep them informed of developments. He knew instinctively that the man who hands out the news gets the advantage in the handling of it. As a result, there was a period when it could be said without documented challenge that he "owned" the editorial pages of the city's principal newspapers. He was much too smart ever to brag about it, either.

In the course of putting through his projects, Moses sometimes had the consent of the elected officials to his operations; other times they just couldn't figure out how to stop him.

I told, in *Politics in the Empire State* how Fiorello La Guardia handled Moses' frequent threats to quit, voiced whenever Moses was being balked on a particular project or approach. La Guardia had the printer rub off a pad of forms reading: "I, Robert Moses, do hereby resign as . . . . . . . . . . effective . . . . . . ." and handed it to Moses one day when Bob was being annoyingly persistent in his "do it my way or else" mood. Moses threw the pad across the room and stamped out of the Mayor's office. He didn't resign from anything, or even threaten to, for at least six months. That, however, was back in 1935 when he was still on the way up.

He staged the scene differently in the crowded reception room of City Hall on January 1, 1954, as Mayor Robert F. Wagner and other members of the incoming administration were being sworn into office. Moses was a key participant because three of the many jobs he held at the moment required new oaths of office administered by a new Mayor. Wagner was willing, in fact happy, to reappoint Moses as

Parks Commissioner and City Construction Coordinator, but he was listening to those in The Establishment who felt that Moses should not be reappointed to the City Planning Commission, where he was able to vote for projects he was sponsoring to the Commission under one of his other hats.

When Moses asked Wagner where the third oath of office was, the latter, anxious as always to avoid a scene, stalled Moses by saying that the clerks had not yet prepared it. Moses acted with characteristic aplomb. He strode back to the clerk's office, seized a blank oath of office, sat down at a typewriter and filled in the blanks for his own reappointment to the planning post. He brought it back triumphantly to the new Mayor. Wagner, his bluff exposed, had no option but to swear Moses in for the third job.

Under the outgoing Mayor Impellitteri, Moses, rather than the Mayor, had dominated the administration. Wagner had been determined that would not happen in his. But at the facedown just narrated, Wagner lost his battle on the day he took office. Moses increased the dimensions of his victory by relating the story of the hand-typed oath to only fifty or so of his most intimate friends, all in city government.

At almost every stage of Moses' career there were those who said that he was growing arrogant, that he was beginning to believe his own laudatory press clippings, that he honestly thought he was infallible. This is too superficial a diagnosis. In my judgment Moses used his proclamations of his own infallibility as a tactical weapon. He could argue, in any dispute, that if he was so right in the past, he was obviously right at the moment. If this theory is correct, it ties up a lot of loose ends in explaining the combination of utter charm and gutter fighter. Those in government who dealt with Moses knew that behind closed doors he was one of the greatest horse traders and compromisers of all time; that he gracefully bowed to as many unpublicized lickings as he scored victories. They also knew that if they challenged and attempted to defeat him out in public, he would fight tooth and nail, by fair means or foul.

The difference seemed to be that a licking in private cost him nothing but the single project he had in mind, but a public defeat, unless met and denounced with all of the vigor and adjectives he could muster, would cost him the public reputation as the man who was always right. Once that foundation was cracked, his whole empire was threatened. So he never publicly admitted a mistake or withdrew an epithet.

Moses' willingness to compromise in private for less than perfection was spelled out by Cleveland Rodgers in a Moses biography published in 1952. Recalling Moses' part in the building of the Triborough Bridge, which had been planned but not started in the Walker administration, Rodgers wrote:

"On the Manhattan side the structure had been planned to land at 125 Street, at least a mile north of the logical location. The Manhattan arm of the bridge should have gone across Ward's Island instead of Randall's, but powerful real estate and business interests had brought about the acquisition of land at 125 Street and Moses had to leave this part of the old plan unchanged to avoid a controversy that might have jeopardized the whole undertaking."

What Rodgers was saying politely was that the approaches at 125 Street had been bought up on the basis of advance information, by William Randolph Hearst and that Moses preferred to build the bridge in the wrong place rather than fight the Hearst newspapers.

How did Moses get started? How did his empire grow?

He entered government, fresh out of Oxford, as a volunteer

worker in the Mitchel administration, working in the Bureau of Municipal Research. This put him in constant contact with influential men like Henry Bruere and George McAneny. At the end of the Mitchel administration, he briefly worked in the War Shipping Administration of World War I. Then Al Smith was elected Governor and appointed a governmental reorganization commission, with his closest adviser, Belle Moskowitz, as secretary. Mrs. Moskowitz, as a rising member of The Establishment, had met Moses, and brought him in as Chief of Staff of the commission. Moses moved completely into the Smith orbit in 1923, when after a single term as Governor, followed by a defeat in the Harding landslide of 1920, Smith was triumphantly returned to Albany for his second term in the 1922 voting.

As Smith began in earnest his previously thwarted program of reorganizing the hodgepodge that had passed up to then as state government, Moses took over as Smith's agent in the area of conservation and state parks, a field close to Smith's heart.

Moses was a doer, a man constantly pressing for action, and he never lost his drive. Through the State Council of Parks and the Long Island State Park Commission, and with Smith's backing, he pushed parkways out into Long Island and created Jones Beach. Both came over the protests of millionnaire estate owners, who pictured Jones Beach as a Coney Island, and the new parkways as deliberate attempts to bring the great unwashed from New York City to their own immaculate doorsteps.

Moses set out to show how great a state-operated public resort could be, and in Jones Beach he scored a triumph he never exceeded.

## Life with Moses

There was always a tendency on Moses' part to embark on dual jobholding, because no one job was ever big enough to keep him busy and therefore happy. He continued to direct the park system while Secretary of State of New York, and left that post only because Franklin Roosevelt, succeeding Smith as Governor, preferred not to have Smith's most active agent in his cabinet.

The policy of the city and state was definitely against allowing a person to hold office on more than one level of government. During the Hylan administration, the President of the Board of Aldermen, Murray Hulbert, innocently accepted honorary, nonsalaried membership on the new Finger Lakes State Park Commission, and the irascible City Controller, Charles L. Craig, cut off Hulbert's salary on the grounds that he had forfeited his city job by taking the state post. The courts upheld Craig, and for the next decade any suggestion of dual officeholding was referred to as giving the man "the finger."

All of this went by the board with the advent of La Guardia, an admirer of Moses, as the city's new Mayor. In rapid succession, in the flush of civic reform and progress:

1. Special legislation in Albany consolidated the city's five borough park departments into one, giving Moses the right to head it by appointment of the Mayor while he still held his state park posts by appointment of the Governor. There was the proviso, however, that he should draw only one salary.

2. In the same spirit he was installed as the driving force in a reconstituted Triborough Bridge Authority that would build the long-planned bridge with the help of a federal

loan. He was not made chairman because of the personal antipathy of the Roosevelt national administration to him, based on an old disagreement.

3. He was also permitted to create the Henry Hudson and Marine Parkway bridge authorities, which turned into rapid moneymakers and whose toll earnings he pyramided into a revolving fund for other projects.

4. As Park Commissioner he managed WPA funds, which paid for serious labor as well as leaf-raking, and with which he was able to build innumerable playgrounds, swimming pools and other recreational facilities.

Every one of the programs was successful and Moses' reputation grew apace. The series of successes also served to change his attitude toward government. In his early years as an advocate of governmental reorganization, particularly in his association with Al Smith, he had argued strenuously and cogently for concentration of government power in the hands of the elected executive, rather than its proliferation in bureaus and agencies several layers removed from direct responsibility to the people. In his new role, he thought differently. Possibly it was because his 1934 candidacy for Governor had convinced him he could never be elected himself; possibly it was because he began to see advantages in getting things done if one were not a candidate for election or re-election.

He had a continuous flow of money coming in from the toll projects, which by 1940 included the Henry Hudson Bridge over the Harlem, the Marine Parkway bridges, the Triborough Bridge and the Midtown Tunnel to Queens. This gave him several choices:

First, he could allow each project to become toll-free as

the cost of its construction was paid off. Second, he could continue the tolls and turn the surplus over to the city treasury, to be spent by the elected public officials for general city purposes. Third, he could keep the income flowing into his office and just build, build, build, without having to ask anyone else, particularly the elected officials, for either tax funds or city credit. Quite understandably, he chose the third course, and having done so, proceeded to protect his position by law.

He had little difficulty in getting legislation in Albany that merged all of the revenue-producing facilities into the Triborough Authority. Few comprehended the importance of the clause in the same bill that gave the Triborough the right to refinance its outstanding debt at any time it saw fit. This worked out as a guarantee of perpetual existence, for whenever a surplus had accumulated, and the debt was in danger of being paid off, Moses would call in the old bonds before their due date, and issue new ones, for fresh money with which to finance new construction.

This was the charter of the Moses empire. From then on, he did not have to truckle to a Borough President to attain his cooperation; he could virtually buy the elected official by waving the money from the Triborough—for his own new projects in the borough, along with the cash for a few pet ideas the Borough President might have. Moses used this power-of-the-purse with characteristic efficiency and gall.

On one occasion, he had quarreled with Borough President James J. Lyons of The Bronx over the details and design of a $23,000,000 rebuilding of Bruckner Boulevard in that borough, which the Triborough had planned to undertake. Moses, withdrawing the funds from The Bronx, rushed to lunch with Borough President John J. Cashmore of Brooklyn and

Since this was still very early in the Wagner administration, and Moses did not feel like denouncing the Mayor, he turned the mimeograph on me and the program. At the same time his representatives asked me to pay no attention to the blast, a request I can only assume was made with his knowledge. Three weeks later, in an executive session of the Board of Estimate, Moses presented the program, along with an additional, nonconflicting program of his own.

Wagner, with a straight face, asked Moses: "Are all of the agencies in agreement?"

Moses, equally bland, replied: "All of the agencies are in agreement."

He then assumed the responsibility for pushing the program through the Legislature.

The mention of "Moses' representatives" requires elaboration. There never was one Robert Moses who single-handedly conducted the day-to-day operations of eight different offices at once. Instead, there was a deputy Robert Moses in each place who handled the detail and brought only important developments or policy problems to the attention of "RM."

Moses, as Park Commissioner, was really a man named Stuart Constable, once the job of being Park Commissioner involved more routine than novelty. The Triborough was run by George E. Spargo; the State Council of Parks by James F. Evans; the State Power Authority by William Chapin, the Slum Clearance Committee by William Lebwohl, and so on.

The City Charter, until its revision in 1961, officially recognized the Moses system of deputies by giving Moses, and Moses alone, the right to vote in the City Planning Commission, though he could designate a representative, so that he would not have to attend the meetings. None of the foregoing is intended to disparage Moses' achievements, merely to explain how one man could seem to be in so many places at one time.

He might spend a day a week at his headquarters in Babylon, on Long Island park and parkway matters, passing on developments, contributing ideas for his underlings, making the key phone call to pin down an agreement or clear up an obstacle. Then he might spend the next few days at his headquarters on Randall's Island, working on Triborough, slum clearance or city construction matters. Or he could be at his third headquarters in the state office building at 270 Broadway, New York City, on state park business or more likely conferring with people who worked downtown, in the City Hall, or Municipal Building, or rented quarters of federal housing and highway agencies. Which office he used for what business mattered not at all except for the convenience it offered at the moment.

Each of Moses' deputies owed and gave unstinting allegiance to "RM." Once a problem had been explored and discussed, it was what *he* wanted that mattered, not what they thought. Once the Moses' policy line had been adopted, no one ever knew what a Moses' deputy thought unless his thoughts were those of Moses himself. In return, every deputy could count on the absolute support of his boss, if his position was ever challenged by any outsider.

Take the conflict which rocked the city in 1959 over whether Joseph Papp's Shakespeare Festival—a new and already loved feature of the city life—would be allowed to continue to present The Bard in Central Park. The Park Department ruled it out and Moses fought Shakespeare tooth and nail until the courts held that the department had been arbitrary in its regulations. The battle did not represent any anti-Shakespeareism in Moses. All that was behind it was that Stuart Constable, the Park deputy for Moses, had gotten into a row, on his own, with Papp, and ordered Papp never to darken the greensward again. As the hassle was public, the rules of the Moses' empire called for Moses to support Constable at all cost, and he did so, unpopular though he made himself for the time.

The influence of the Moses empire overflowed even its recognized boundaries because architects, engineers and administrators spawned within it, moved, with Moses' sanction, to government posts in other areas. They remained Moses men. A conspicuous example was provided by the New York City Housing Authority, with which Moses never had any formal connection, but successive chairmen and chief engineers of that agency came up through the Moses school and still regarded him as their boss.

In his push to accomplish so much, Moses developed a bland disregard for such technical amenities of government as Civil Service employment lists, competitive bidding, or allocation of costs. He thus ran an elastic establishment that could take on a major new assignment without setting up a provision for overhead directly attributable thereto; could be started in motion without delay. Ad hoc assignments such as the Slum Clearance Committee or the work of the City Construction Coordinator, which had no statutory standing, were duck soup for Moses, while they would have been headaches for anyone else to take on. A man whose salary was being paid by Triborough or Parks could easily spend most of his time on Slum Clearance or Construction Coordinators work.

# Life with Moses

It was all so free and easy that it sometimes staggered the onlooker. I recall that on one occasion, Mayor Wagner promised Moses he would remove the Vice-Chairman of the Slum Clearance Committee—who was in Moses' doghouse at the moment—and appoint a new Moses' selection. When the Mayor had second thoughts, and did not make the change, Moses effected it himself by simply printing new stationery for the agency, with the new man's name in place of the old.

In the same freewheeling way, he adopted architects, landscape experts, engineers and construction firms and used them on project after project, with no one else invited. The pay or contracts they got were negotiated by Moses as if he were running a private rather than governmental show. Working consistently with the same team had many advantages for Moses. However, if anyone else had tried the same thing, auditing and investigating agencies would have broken down the doors for a look at the books and to ask why public bidding had not been sought. But since it was Moses, and his personal honesty was never in question, no one did.

Somewhere in his career Moses developed complete contempt for the dollar sign—the cost of things. It probably stemmed from the WPA era, when the whole object was to spend as much money as fast as possible to keep people from unemployment and starvation. He reconstructed Bryant Park with WPA funds, turning an eyesore in the heart of New York into a fine park, where grass and trees grew for the first time. It led to the quip that "only Bob can grow a tree." Few realized that Moses and the WPA rebuilt Bryant Park not once, but three times, before they achieved success. The trees were important then, the money wasn't.

Later this policy of ignoring the ultimate cost involved much greater sums. He might plan a highway which could be built to minimum standards for $20,000,000, and to proper standards for $30,000,000. If only the $20,000,000 were available, or if he was going to run into opposition, for other reasons, to a maximum effort, he had no hesitancy in going ahead with the $20,000,000 project. When it proved inadequate, he would rebuild it later, at the cost of another $20,000,000, spending $40,000,000 all told for what $30,000,000 would have bought originally. But he might also have had to wait, and he always preferred not to. Much as Moses deserves credit as a pioneer in the building of parks and highways around New York, so does he deserve demerits for the hasty construction and poor planning which made so many of them unsatisfactory and unequal to the tasks for which they were intended. The Long Island Expressway was only one of many which fell into this category.

To those who thought of city planning in terms of ivory tower expertise, Moses was a constant thorn. His approach was to look for and discover some area in the city that needed, in his opinion, a face-lifting. Then he would scout around for a reason to go to work on it. He decided to rebuild Columbus Circle before he thought of the Colisseum as its showplace, and he mentally moved in on Lincoln Square, six blocks north on Broadway, before he thought up the Lincoln Center for the arts.

The same technique backfired when he looked over the crowded area south of Washington Square, filled with old houses, and decided that the only way to redevelop it was to cut a broad roadway through Washington Square and continue Fifth Avenue as Fifth Avenue South. The old Italian community to the south, and the Greenwich Villagers to the east and west—as articulate and persistent groups as could be found anywhere, not only defeated a widened roadway through the Park, but secured the closing of the old one, from the vote-conscious elected officials to whom they appealed. At the time of the battle, Moses wasn't quite sure what he would build if he won, but the whole question became moot.

Moses' greatest consistent successes were scored in the development of parks, although he was less interested in maintaining them than creating them. His weakest batting average was in the field of housing, which he attempted to make his own. My own feeling on this is that Moses always had great empathy with the people en masse, but little, if any at all, for the problems of the individual. This showed the most in housing, where people had to be moved out of old buildings to make way for the new.

The massive public housing program in New York City, interrupted by World War II, was resumed immediately thereafter, with Moses supervising it as City Construction Coordinator. The city not only had a critical shortage of decent housing, but unlike other cities, it suffered also from a dearth of substandard housing, slum buildings which could be used for temporary occupancy by the people the new construction displaced.

Thousands of new apartments were rushed into construction as the old slums were demolished. Those who had lived in the slums were shifted from one condemned building to another, even abandoned military barracks. No effective system of relocation existed; maybe none was possible at the time. Moses went full steam ahead as if the relocation problem wasn't even there.

The bulldozer approach—which involved the tearing down of everything in an area—was the only one used and public housing projects were built so big that they were in effect whole neighborhoods in themselves. Other errors were made such as ignoring the existence of large families and elderly couples, for whom the new projects had no accommodations.

The Moses reputation survived all of this, since his responsibility was indirect, but it rocked under a series of blows in connection with housing for which Moses had a direct, public connection—the Title I program carried on by him through his chairmanship of the Slum Clearance Committee. The mistakes there marked the beginning of the end of the Moses empire. "Title I" was governmental shorthand for the first section of a federal housing law and the one that provided federal funds to help in slum clearance and urban renewal. Under it, the city could acquire large built-up areas that needed rehabilitation, then sell them off for a new use, with the city and federal government treasuries sharing the loss. Elsewhere in the United States under the same program, the land was acquired, cleared and the public authorities then invited bids for new use.

Moses, probably because he was afraid cleared land might be preempted by some agency or program too big to lick, always insisted on signing up the new use first, before anything was torn down. He also insisted on personally selecting the "sponsor" who would erect the new buildings on the property given to him at a low cost. The new use was not limited to low cost or rent-controlled projects; it often involved a combination of commercial use and high rent residential space. The Colisseum is an example of the mixed use.

But Moses picked the sponsors with the same disregard for the forms and amenities that he chose his engineers and construction firms for parks and bridges, and in several cases he tripped badly.

In the case of one West Side development, the sponsors took over the property, with a very small investment, and made more money just collecting the slum rentals than they would have by investing millions in new buildings. So they never demolished, and Moses, reluctant as ever to admit he had made a mistake, prodded them privately but never forced them out.

In the case of other Title I projects, where old low rental housing was demolished, the new buildings rented at very high rates, rather than at the middle-income level which the public and the city officialdom had expected.

Eventually, every mistake that had been made was aired by the newspapers, and Moses and Mayor Wagner were under fire for the "Title I scandal." It took a long time for the Mayor to move, but when he did, the Slum Clearance Committee went down the drain, replaced by a new, all-encompassing Housing and Redevelopment Board. Moses was no longer sitting in the drivers' seat in the housing field, and he, for the first time, had had a job taken away from him.

The change attracted less comment than might have been expected, because it came when Moses was about to move in as head of the 1964 World's Fair, several years in advance of the opening, and he resigned voluntarily from a number of other city posts to avoid a conflict of interest between the public positions and the private Fair employment.

But what was not printed at all was that when Moses resigned as City Parks Commissioner, in this period, he tried and failed to get Mayor Wagner to name a Moses' deputy as his successor. Wagner was quite pleased with himself for the way he handled it without arousing a Moses' explosion.

Wagner told Moses that the deputy might actually be as able as Moses contended, but that nobody knew of the man.

"With the national and worldwide reputation that you have, Bob," said the Mayor, "do you really think it would be a compliment to you if I named a complete unknown to succeed you."

Moses found no counter to the Mayor's argument.

He still had enough, along with the Fair, to keep him busy. Even without the city jobs, he remained Chairman of Triborough, Chairman of the New York State Power Authority, Chairman of the State Council of Parks, President of the Long Island State Park Commission, and unsalaried city representative in dealing with the state and federal governments on the arterial highway program within the city.

But his star was on the wane, and those who might not have tackled him as an opponent years before were less reluctant to do so. In early 1963, the newly reelected Governor Nelson Rockefeller decided to replace Moses as Chairman of the State Council of Parks to make room for the Governor's brother, Laurance, who had served for years as Vice-Chairman. Rockefeller, in letters to Moses, indicated that he was planning for the future and thus implied that Moses might not be around forever. Moses, in fury, resigned every other state post he held.

No matter what happened later between Moses and Mayor Lindsay, the Rockefeller action signified the end. The indispensable man had reached the dispensable state.

---

* The list (on facing page 213), set up as it is by decades, omits Moses' chairmanship of the early Henry Hudson and Marine Parkway Authorities, merged into the Triborough in the 1930's, a brief period as Chairman of the City Planning Commission in the 1940's, and his presidency of the World's Fair of 1964 and 1965.

† Removed, July 12, 1966.

# Life with Moses

## The Moses Empire

*A listing of his multiple jobs in each decade, working back from the current years**

| 1936 | 1946 | 1956 | 1966 |
|---|---|---|---|
| Commissioner of Parks of New York City | Commissioner of Parks of New York City | Commissioner of Parks of New York City | |
| Triborough Bridge Authority, secretary and chief executive officer | Triborough Bridge Authority, Chairman | Triborough Bridge and Tunnel Authority, Chairman | Triborough Bridge and Tunnel Authority, Chairman |
| State Council of Parks, Chairman | State Council of Parks, Chairman | State Council of Parks, Chairman | |
| L. I. State Park Commission, President | L. I. State Park Commission, President | L. I. State Park Commission, President | |
| | New York City Tunnel Authority, secretary and chief executive officer | (merged into Triborough) | |
| | City Construction Coordinator | City Construction Coordinator † | |
| | City Planning Commission, Member | City Planning Commission, Member | |
| | | New York State Power Authority, Chairman | |
| | | New York City Slum Clearance Committee, Chairman | |
| | | New York City Youth Board, Member | |

213

# 11. The Great Society

The advent of Lyndon B. Johnson's Great Society had its impact on all of the cities of the nation. In New York, with its long history of social pioneering, the Great Society approach was less than revolutionary as a concept; in fact, in some aspects it was even old hat. But coming as it did after the preparatory eras of the New Deal, the Fair Deal and the New Frontiers of Johnson's Democratic predecessors in the White House, it gave further impetus to political changes already in the works, and increased political ferment.

Philosophically the Johnson program endorsed the idea that it was proper for the federal government to make direct cash contributions designed to upgrade the living and cultural standards of everybody while simultaneously trying to close the gap in existence between the haves and the have nots. In scope its objectives were clearly larger than those outlined or attempted by anyone in authority in the past, anywhere in the United States.

But as an approach to some problems of government it had been almost routine in New York City and State for forty years—ever since Al Smith, as Governor, established the first broad formula for state aid to education. The Smith program was simple. The rich as well as the poor communities of the state were evaluated as to their relative wealth—in terms of real estate values—and the state gave them cash for educational purposes to the extent that they were not rich enough to pay by themselves for the new standards the state was setting up at the time for decent school buildings and adequate pay for teachers. Since New York City was the wealthiest community by the real estate measuring rod, it got the least in aid. Again because it was the wealthiest in business and industry, it paid most of the state tax monies used to finance the program. Smith made no bones about asking the New York City residents to help finance the education of the children of places they had never heard of, like Penn Yan, Mechanicville or Rouses Point, so that they could have opportunities at least equal to those then given the children of New York City. He sold the concept than an uneducated or poorly educated child anywhere in the state was as much a liability to the city as if he lived within its borders.

What was remarkable about the Smith program was that it came without the thirty years of groundwork that preceded the Johnson approach and it remained popular in New York City, which paid the bill for it.

Of course, almost everything Smith did was popular in New York City. It never gave him less than a rousing majority every time he ran. He spent, or planned the spending, of hundreds of millions for state parks and institutions. When he was defeated once in the great GOP landslide of 1920, he was welcomed back with open arms two years later, after two years of penny-pinching and tax reduction by the Republican Nathan L. Miller. This illustrates as well as anything that no one wins an election in New York City on an economy platform. By 1966 the talk of economy in government was a rarity before, during or after a political campaign. In the campaign itself, the closest the intelligent office seeker would come to an economy pledge was to indicate that he thought there could be "savings" in the operation of government so that the tax monies could purchase more services.

In the light of that background, it is worthwhile taking a look at the effect of the Great Society approach on services, taxes, state and federal aid, the political establishment, and the relative prestige of local, state and federal politicians.

## SERVICES

Services were the keynote to political success in New York for a decade before the Johnson election. The Great Society program simply added emphasis to demands that had already appeared insatiable. For example, the original subway system went without a police force of its own for half a century. The more recent Housing Authority had a small force of watchmen, which it paid for itself out of its rental income or federal and state subsidies. As demands grew for additional protection in these areas, the city furnished funds, the forces were trained and uniformed, and doubled in number. Then they were doubled again, and again, until each by itself ranked among the larger police forces of the nation.

The city started lighting playgrounds at night following the outcry after a particularly nasty gang killing had taken place in an unlighted one. It wound up by re-lighting the streets of the whole city. A foundation grant sparked a program of volunteer workers in the public schools. In a few years the city had not only assumed the responsibility for the program, but had expanded it and also, separately, hired neighborhood mothers as paid teacher aides. The free Shakespeare Festival, privately financed, was a success in Central Park, so the city acceded to the request that it carry the same program into the schools. These, and countless more, were deservedly popular, and only occasionally did the demands reach the ludicrous, as they did in connection with playgrounds.

In 1954 there was a demand for more playgrounds, and over the years it was met by building hundreds more. But by 1964 the same pressure groups were back in City Hall to have the playgrounds lined with rubber or tanbark, so that little Willie wouldn't be hurt if he fell.

Generally the expansion of work in the social welfare and cultural fields was so popular that once a new program was started, and was successful, it was certain to obtain city support on an expanded basis, either because the administration thought it was a good idea or because it couldn't fight the do-gooders and win. It reached the point that a Mayor could usually achieve his budget ends simply by listing the areas that proposals for appropriation cutting would affect.

The economy-minded made a stab at cutting the expenses of local government without cutting services shortly before the Wagner administration took office in 1953. They had persuaded O'Dwyer, during his regime, to sponsor a major study, carried out by a high-level Mayor's Committee on Management Survey, and directed by the distinguished expert, Luther Gulick. The survey took several years and when it was completed in the spring of 1953, Dr. Gulick predicted that if the management practices he proposed were put into effect, the city could save $75,000,000 a year. The prospect was widely applauded.

# The Great Society

Mayor-elect Wagner saw the possibility of the savings' prophecy hanging around his neck, with continuing queries in the years ahead by hostile press and pressure groups if he failed to save the $75,000,000 a year. His solution was worthy of a minor league Machiavelli. He simply created the office of City Administrator—as the survey had urged—to oversee the management practices of the city, and he persuaded Dr. Gulick to accept the post. The Mayor's point was that if Dr. Gulick couldn't save the $75,000,000, after thinking up the ways to do it, who could?

As things worked out, Dr. Gulick was an able and valuable city servant who pushed successfully for the adoption by the city of new and needed city services, and the expansion of existing ones. What he and the administration did in this connection was plainly visible. However, the savings that were supposed to stem from the improved management practices never became visible. Putting the new practices into effect cost money at the start and any savings from them were gobbled up by increased spending concepts. A perfect example was the Gulick-sponsored career and salary plan for city employees. It certainly improved the caliber of city service, particularly at the middle, career level, and by increasing efficiency, could be said to have promoted economy. But the salaries of those same employees increased visibly and astronomically.

So, at this point, a decade before the advent of the Great Society, the responsible proponents of economy in government gave up the ghost. They stopped even talking about ways to cut costs and were willing to settle for anything that would diminish the pace at which the costs increased each year. The civic and business leaders who in prior years might have been battling for economy and private action began leading fights for the preservation of Carnegie Hall or the creation of Lincoln Center as more in keeping with the times, and no one balked at the use of city funds for the purpose. Thus when the Great Society came on the scene in New York, there was no limiting its fields of action.

## TAXES

A major reason frequently cited for the popularity, and therefore political desirability, of the spending approach to government in New York City is that its tax structure, up to the Lindsay administration, was largely invisible to the great majority of its voters. They are rent payers rather than home owners, so they have no continuing awareness of increases in the real estate tax, which not only contributes to the running expenses, but is stuck with the entire job of paying for borrowings for capital improvements. They are equally oblivious to the various business taxes buried in commercial overhead, but which figure in the price of what the residents use or buy. On the other hand, they were always extremely conscious of subway and bus fare increases, of which they had reminders at least twice a day.

The voters lack what is so commonplace in rural America —the direct connection between new spending and higher taxes in the form of tax bills presented directly to them. However, the fault for this lies as much with the public as with the politicians. A city income tax was proposed by the politicians and howled down by the public as long ago as 1932. So was a proposal to charge ten-cent tolls on the existing toll-free interborough bridges. In the 1950's there was a ten-cent-per-ride tax on taxicab use, rejected loudly by the public, with the help of the cab drivers, and repealed within a few months. All through the 1950's there was a direct city tax on auto registrations, but the auto clubs had received commitments it would be repealed, and it was, as soon as the city could bludgeon equivalent revenue from the state.

The one major direct tax the city ever imposed up to 1966 was the sales tax, originally levied in 1934 at the low rate of one percent and earmarked then to pay the cost of home relief in the bottom of the depression. At its outset it was resented by few, for most of those who paid were happy to have the money to spend on taxable items. By 1965, when it had become a combined state-city tax, and was levied at five percent, which covered new areas such as services, it was regarded for the first time as a political liability.

The need for new tax sources for the city to meet increased employee payrolls and demands for new and better public services turned the decade 1954 through 1964 into a continuing tax hunt. At one stage the Wagner administration let itself be prodded into a private survey of taxes elsewhere to see if there were any revenue-producing ones that New York had overlooked. The survey did turn up a city in Kansas that had in effect a head tax on gasoline pumps. Every other tax in every other city or state had already been put into effect here or had been considered and already rejected as unsuitable or politically suicidal.

Wagner, in his last year in office, gave up trying to find new taxes or raising old ones, and just borrowed to meet his budget deficit. This compounded the problems of his successor, for it put a mortgage of one year's normal budget increase, $300,000,000 on a potential increase in the real estate tax, leaving Mayor Lindsay further away from meeting his own deficits.

With no end in sight for the demand on services, the city

had turned first to the state government and later to the
federal government, for financial assistance, even before it
ran out of its own tax resources. A strong drive to obtain tax
monies out of the state came in the 1950's, out of the federal
government in the 1960's. The appeals were made publicly
in the name of equity, and privately for the sake of political
expediency, but on either ground they had merit. The city's
great concentration of industry, management offices and
finance made it the largest tax base in the nation, contributing
far more than any other place to both federal and state revenues. If the city was fresh out of tax sources, it was because
the other levels had pulled their superior rank and preempted
the most profitable and least painful source. Politically it had
always been held proper to try to get someone else to levy
taxes and take whatever criticism resulted. New York City
administrations preferred tax action by the Governor and
the Legislature in Albany, or the President and Congress in
Washington, particularly when they began to run out of tax
ideas.

A ten-year propaganda campaign waged by the city did
produce two new revenue sources. The first was a share of
the state gasoline and auto license fees, most of which funds
were neutralized by the city carrying out its prior pledge to
repeal its own auto use tax if it received the revenues it was
entitled to from the state. The second was the transfer to
the city of the entire state revenue from the stock transfer
tax, which the city had been claiming for years was its by
superior right of services rendered. But to get it, the city
had to sign away to to the state the fourth cent of its own
sales tax, in the course of a merger of the old city and the
new state sales tax. It did obtain vastly increased appropriations or allowances from the state to spend in the fields of

education, health, hospitals and corrections. Worthy as these were in their social results they boomeranged financially. Every time the city was given another $25,000,000 a year in the form of state aid for education, it felt obliged, in antici- pation of public pressure, to match the new state money with additional city funds. The financial equities were such that the city could legitimately have cut its appropriation by the amount of new states funds, or not added any of its own. But the demand for higher education appropriations was so great that no Mayor dared try it. He would have had to face too many angry mothers, teacher groups, and editorial critics.

The same situation existed, with a lower boiling point on the part of the public, in the case of new state aid for mental health, housing, urban renewal, parole and probation, water and air pollution control, so each new batch of state money evoked new city money as well. The later turn to the federal government produced no better budgetary assistance. The federal assistance was almost invariably in the form of capital outlay money, or specific grants for new programs. I can recall not a single federal appropriation that relieved the city of costs it had been bearing.

## FEDERAL-STATE ASSISTANCE

There had always been—even before the Great Society— a substantial drawback attached to the use of federal or state contributions for a locally operated program. It is the old story that the man who pays the fiddler calls the tune. In terms of administration, policy and planning, any city project or program that is aided by state or federal funds automati- cally is controlled by the higher echelon of government. All the state or federal agency has to say—and frequently does—is "if you want to do it that way, you can't use our money."

Sometimes this paternal approach works out for the best, sometimes for the worst, but in every case it produces delays and red tape while the bureaucracy at each level of government passes on every detail. Sometimes the policy conflicts produce ludicrous results.

For example, one year Congress attached a rider to an appropriation bill for federal housing monies requiring every family living in a federally-aided project to sign a loyalty oath denying any connection with the Communist party. In New York City this would have required that the operating and construction agency, the Housing Authority, had to collect affidavits from the 30,000 families living in projects financed out of federal bond issues but none from the 60,000 families living in projects paid for out of state or city bond issues. In fact, if the agency had tried to comply with the federal law, it would have been using state funds without authority.

On another occasion, bathing rather than loyalty was involved, and the conflict was between the state and the city. The Authority had been trying for years to include showers in the bathtubs in the projects it built for the state. It conceded that the installation costs would be greater, but that the hot-water usage would be appreciably less, and besides that, ignoring the existence of showers in the middle 1950's in buildings due to last another fifty years seemed less than farsighted. The state insisted that its money could not, and would not, be used for the purpose. Then along came a project that the city felt should be built in the form of four fourteen-story buildings. The state wanted three buildings, nineteen stories high, housing the same number of apartments, at a total cost of $85,000 less. The way it was compromised was that the city accepted the state's plan for the three buildings, with the $85,000 to be spent on showers and with a commitment of showers in all future state projects. Even at the time, it hardly seemed a high standard for decision-making.

The stories of unnecessary paper work could go on forever. One that cannot be omitted involved the requirement of the federal government that the executive director of the Housing Authority sign 12 copies of an affidavit, every time the authority bought stoves or refrigerators certifying that the purchase had not been disapproved at a referendum of the people of the State of New York. It happened that the state constitution, required to be on file with the federal bureaucrats, did not even permit referenda of that kind. But the federal government even rejected a compromise of one original signature, plus 11 rubber-stamped facsimiles until the executive director threatened to carry the paper war to the press.

There have been similar rhubarbs all through the years, in the administration of welfare, where the city does the work but most of the costs are borne by the state and federal governments and by virtually every other multi-agency financed program. They were increasingly visible in the Great Society in programs involving the war on poverty, legal defense, and others.

The logical solution is one whereby the federal government would allocate a share of its taxing powers and revenues to the localities, rather than handing out the funds after collection. But this would require Congress to give up its role as Santa Claus.

# The Great Society

The governmental pressures involved in the Great Society were reflected almost from the start. There had been a time when the line of promotion for a bright young man was well established. He started as an Alderman or Assemblyman, was promoted to the State Senate, and finally the best or the luckiest could count on a seat on the bench or a place on the statewide ticket. By the mid-1960's, the road skipped Albany. A City Councilman, already endowed with more prestige than his aldermanic predecessor, made headway faster by steering directly for Washington, with a seat in the House of Representatives and his hopes fixed on an eventual place in the United States Senate.

Several reasons for this are worth noting. First, the trend reflects not only the increase in importance of the federal government, but a corresponding decline in the attractiveness of Albany as a base of operations. The aspiring politico who once had been elected to the Legislature could, if he wanted to, make his name in the field of broad policy, and skip annoying details. After all, New York City was stuck with the nasty municipal housekeeping jobs, and the state was not. With increased urbanization of all of the sixty-two counties and sixty-two cities, the housekeeping is now a state job as well. The state no longer can look the other way on administration and overseeing of the legislation it passes, since the pressure for action now comes from both parties and all directions, instead of from New York City alone.

More recently the men in Albany have had to become involved not only at the high policy level but at the lower detailed planning level, in areas such as the location of highways, the quality and quantity of subsidized train service, of sewage disposal, water supply, and anything else that figures in urban living. This is less than a political gold mine, for no matter how much an elected public official may proclaim his accomplishments in the solid areas of meeting or trying to meet absolute needs, the public shows its awareness only when the trains are late or stop running, when the sewer overflows, or the water doesn't.

A second, possibly temporary factor, is the increased uncertainty of tenure of a seat in the State Legislature. The "one man, one vote" decision of the United States Supreme Court upset ancient legislative apportionments everywhere. It was certainly an advantage in the long run to New York City, constitutionally under-represented since 1894. But in working out new district lines, first there was a temporary apportionment set up by the old Legislature, then there was a second imposed by the federal courts, and a third loomed up as the probable result of a 1967 state constitutional convention. Legislative lines were obliterated, local ties destroyed, just in the same period when the Reform movement in the Democratic party was hitting the old-time representatives from one direction, and increased demands from Negro and Puerto Rican groups for their fair share of representation was coming from another. No legislator, no matter what his record, was safe in his seat, the way he had been, and the uncertainty served to make the career in Albany just one more bit less attractive.

The deterioration of Albany prestige was progressive as a result. The legislative shakeups did not bring consistently better replacements, though they did produce some bright and able young men. The stability stemming from tenure and solid organization backing at home was missing. There was also an increased scramble for space in the newspapers, a race to be the most spectacular, rather than the solidest, forced in part by the fact that the papers had already cut down their Albany news to make room for increased news from Washington and abroad.

The prestige of the governorship also went downhill. There was a time when just being Governor of New York almost insured nomination for the Presidency by one of the major parties. In writing *Politics in the Empire State* in the winter of 1947, I said:

> . . . in the twenty presidential elections from the end of the Civil War through 1944, there have been fourteen campaigns in which at least one of the principal nominees was a New Yorker. In two of them both major-party nominees called New York home . . . . There was Horatio Seymour and then Horace Greeley in the first two elections after the death of Lincoln. Then came Tilden who carried New York and the nation but was counted out by an electoral commission. Cleveland ran three times. There were Teddy Roosevelt and Alton B. Parker in 1904, with T.R. again as a Progressive in 1912. Then came Hughes and Al Smith, Franklin Roosevelt four times in a row, with Tom Dewey as his opponent in FDR's last campaign . . . All but Greeley and Parker had previously been elected Governor of New York; they had shown their parties the vote-getting strength that seemed to justify the conclusion that if nominated for the presidency, they would have at least an even chance of adding to their party's column the state's cherished electoral votes. What it amounts to is that every Governor of New York is ex officio a potential presidential nominee unless barred constitutionally by foreign birth or practically, by racial or religious consideration.*

* *Politics in the Empire State*, Warren Moscow, Alfred A. Knopf Inc., New York.

Dewey was nominated for the second time in 1948, but no New York Governor has been the nominee of either major party in the four elections since that date. Averell Harriman tried hard as a Democrat in 1956 and Nelson Rockefeller as a Republican in 1960 and 1964, but neither came close. This was ironic because each of them had deliberately sought the governorship as a stepping-stone to the presidency. They would have done better trying for the United States Senate.

Prior to World War II the nation, as well as New York, had the well-established habit of turning to its governors rather than its senators for its presidential possibilities. In the years that followed there was a slow but steady shift, visible first when Richard Nixon was picked for the Vice Presidency in 1952, and Estes Kefauver by the Democrats in their losing 1956 campaign for the same office. By 1960 the nominees for President and Vice President of both major parties—Kennedy-Johnson and Nixon-Lodge, had made their reputations in Congress, rather than in a state house, and this was repeated in 1964 with the Johnson-Humphrey and Goldwater-Miller slates.

It does not mean that an outstanding Governor will no longer be considered for the presidency. It does mean that the increased emphasis on Washington as the seat of important government gives the Senator the edge over the Governor, reversing the historic situation.

Within the city itself, membership in the City Council also has suddenly become more important in the 1960's. The framers of the 1937 charter, which abolished the old 65-member Board of Aldermen and created a smaller Council, used much language to increase the theoretical powers of the Council, but the authority of the Mayor and the Board of Estimate was simultaneously continued as it had been, so that the

Council remained a rubber stamp. It suffered also from the fact that for ten years its members were elected by proportional representation which was stacked in favor of demagogues, blatherskites and the Communists. The system worked that way because it provided no means of voting against, or defeating, a candidate who the great majority of the people felt was unfit. The charter revision of 1961 increased the power of the Mayor, and virtually deprived the Board of Estimate of the real control it had had over legislation and policy so that the Council, elected on a saner basis was left as the city's local unicameral legislature.

The general picture, in the Johnson Great Society, was of city and federal governments, and their political operators, reaching out to each other, ignoring the state lines that once had dominated both the governments and the politicians. New York was no exception.

# 12.  The Political Climate

New York's politicians and officeholders operate in a political climate that is as demanding and confusing as anything outside of Washington, D.C. Part of this comes from the voter whose attitude toward the city's political system is akin to that of the jealous wife, who always hopes for the best and fears for the worst. In loose conversation, the voter is certain that all politicians and officeholders are crooked, yet he will exculpate, when pressed, each and every one familiar to him. He resents special privilege—for others. He knows he can't get a traffic ticket fixed because a fix-proof ticket system was installed as far back as 1950, but he remains certain that others with "pull" can arrange it for themselves. He gripes daily about the rush-hour crowds in the subway, and wonders why someone hasn't arranged to stagger the working hours for people in other occupations. He thinks sincerely that the city is going to pot and not even the new building construction, over which he has been tripping constantly for years, can convince him otherwise. He thinks the city is dirty, compared with others he has visited or heard of, but doesn't connect that with the cigarette butt that he invariably tosses into the street. He is so completely normal in these manifestations of the danger inherent in a little bit of learning that the difference between him and the citizens elsewhere is hard to spot. It lies in his attitude toward the city in which he lives.

The citizen of any place else brags about his home town, lists its cultural attractions, defends it against attack or justifies its shortcomings when they can't be ignored. The New Yorker, native or transplant, takes the virtues and assets of the most amazing city in the world so much for granted that he never mentions them. He is clear and loud only in his complaints.

New York has always been Mecca for touring Americans, and for the young and ambitious seeking glamour and success, but the attraction the city has for them is not based on sales talks by its residents. When Newbold Morris died in 1966 after thirty-five years as a conscientious and sincere, though not dazzling public official, the press referred to his feeling for New York as his "love affair" with the city. They thought it unique, and were close to being right. Yet Morris was far more justified in his attitude toward the city than either the press or the rest of the people. It has more to commend it than its skyline, its theaters, stores and museums, its crowds and its worldliness. Ignoring all these, New York would still stand out among the cities of America for its high standards of public service, governmental efficiency, and even political morality.

Consider services. Any study of government operations elsewhere always shows that New York stands high, but is not tops, in everything. There is always a single city that surpasses New York in its services in some one field, though it is inferior in the others. There is no city that rivals New York in overall services—such things as the frequency of garbage collection, the twenty-four-hour transit system, housing efforts, concern over the safety of the elevators—which make New York possible—fire-fighting and emergency equipment.

In all these and countless others, New York's superior standards and efforts are hidden by the immensity of the problems created by the city's density, the fight for space in the heart of the city. Take traffic. It is a cinch to keep traffic flowing smoothly through the main streets of a city that boasts of possibly one thirty-story "tower" dominating the four-story buildings that make up the rest of its business district. That represents no density problem at all.

But in New York the forty-story buildings which are as commonplace as the four-story structures elsewhere, attract at least ten times as many pedestrians, autos, taxis, service trucks and delivery vans as the four-story buildings with the equivalent street frontage. The trouble in New York's garment center stems not from the width of the streets, but from the capacity of the elevators within the buildings, which slows the loading or unloading time. The fact that New York's streets year after year handle a steadily increasing flow, and still are choked no worse than in the days of the horse-drawn van, is a tribute to the effort that has been put into traffic direction and control. Yet the citizen grumbles that the problem has not been solved.

Then there is water supply. A century or more ago the city reached out beyond its own boundaries for new and better sources after its own shallow wells were no longer adequate. The Hudson is tidal and salty for 60 miles north, so New York first tapped the Croton River in Westchester, then bought up half of Putnam County for reservoirs for both supply and storage. Later it tunnelled under the increasingly polluted Hudson to bring new water from the Catskills and finally it stretched out to the headwaters of the Delaware.

All of the territory it included in its watershed received the guarantee that the city would forever protect the source of supply against pollution; it would furnish the locality water from the reservoirs it built and would charge no more for that water than it charged its own citizens. In the case of the cities along the Delaware in three other states, it guaranteed to keep the Delaware flowing for them, in summer drought, by releasing from its reservoirs the spring flood waters it stored annually. It produced the best water in America from the point of view of purity and taste, and it also furnished the most, meeting a peak demand of 1,200,000,000 gallons a day.

It was a marvellous achievement, accepted by the citizenry without comment. Then came a drought that in 1966 had lasted for five years and affected the entire Northeast. The city cut down on water usage first, by a campaign of public education, and then by moderate restrictions on use. The press, to show how bad New York's system was, held up Philadelphia as a shining example, ignoring the fact that if New York had not built storage dams on the upper Delaware, Philadelphia's pipes into the river would have been pulling in water that was saline. Another reaction was that a candidate for the nomination for Mayor, known only in his home area, got city-wide publicity for a week and 100,000 votes on Primary Day, when he posed for pictures at a waterleak.

It seemed to some that the city administration should have pointed with pride to its water accomplishments; should have boasted that the city still had water despite the unprecedented drought while other cities were at the crisis stage; that there was nothing wrong with New York's water planning that a single year of normal rainfall wouldn't straighten out. The administration—with a base in sad experience—felt that the public would never accept the accomplishments of the previous decade or the previous century as an excuse for the short-age of the moment. They quoted, as politicians are prone to do with a monotonous ritualism, the hypothetical story of the constituent and the politician who chided him for ingratitude.

The voter, according to the story, acknowledged all past favors and added, "But what have you done for me lately?"

Consider moral standards. The assumption of corruption among New York politicians ignores the fact that wrong-doing is a human rather than a local phenomenon, and that if New York is an exception in the field, it is because its trend is more in the direction of righteousness. New York, without a reform wave, has standards higher than other cities in the full flush of temporary civic virtue. I recall a taxi ride in an-other big city, during a national political convention, from the hall to the principal hotel headquarters. As the cab neared the hotel in the heart of town, the driver handed a quarter to the policeman in the middle of the street directing traffic. When I questioned him he explained that unless he gave the policeman the quarter, he would not have been allowed to steer his car into the hotel "feed line" where he would pick up another fare, and that he had not been singled out, but all of the drivers paid.

That city was in the first year of an acclaimed reform ad-ministration. The political convention to which it was host had been eagerly sought to provide the new administration with a showcase in which to parade its virtues. Yet everyone took it for granted that a policeman could still exact graft from the taxi drivers in broad daylight at the busiest intersec-tion in town.

In New York that kind of open petty thievery wouldn't exist. The taxi drivers would picket City Hall, the Police Commissioner would be called on the carpet and the policemen involved would be fired. Of course there are New York City policemen who take graft, but the political climate does not condone it, and it involves small rewards for considerable risk.

New York public's willingness to suspect the worst poses a problem even for the honest officeholder. In 1964 Paul Screvane was President of the City Council, next in line for the mayoralty, and an aspirant for the post the following year, if Wagner didn't run. He was tipped off that he was being accused of having taken a sizable bribe. The story was percolating through the notoriously corrupt parking meter industry that the parking meter company that had just gotten a big contract from the city owed its success to a $50,000 payment to Screvane. No money had been paid to Screvane or anyone else in the city administration, though the practice was common enough elsewhere. Screvane's dilemma was whether he should ignore the rumor and thus limit its circulation, or blow the whistle for the cops to catch up with the malefactor, a step which would spread the report and provoke city-wide gossip. He called in the District Attorney instantly, but paid the price for it. After ten months of grand jury investigation and newspaper headlines linking his name with bribe rumors, and a public trial of the man actually guilty, Screvane was cleared completely. What had happened was that a man associated with the company had told the manufacturer he needed $50,000 for Screvane to get the contract, and then he pocketed the fee himself. He pleaded guilty, but Screvane's own campaign for the mayoralty limped along under a severe handicap until the clearance came, inevitably belated.

Another problem for the officeholders, particularly acute since World War II, stems from the fact that meeting the public clamor for civic progress necessarily involves moving citizens and voters off the site of the proposed improvement, be it a highway, bridge, hospital or school. And no one who hadn't planned to move likes the city telling him he has to do so.

Politicians, in the middle of public upheaval, have a tendency to duck if they have no solution. So the reshuffling of the population's living quarters in the last twenty years has lacked consistent political leadership. The men in office have been for progress in principle, while ostensibly opposing the inconveniencing of hundreds or thousands of citizens in the act of raising merry hell. The problem arises because few members of the irate public and only a minority of the officeholders appreciate the importance of the pattern of change.

One facet of the change has been the departure of the manufacturing industry from the city limits. The politicians, the press and the public unite in mourning its loss, with the press and the public convinced that the exodus can be laid at the door of the government. They blame taxes imposed by the city, or labor conditions inherent in statewide laws. Actually, manufacturing moves out because the city can no longer afford the space for it, no matter what the taxes or the union rules.

It has been physically displaced by the business of management. The men who run the manufacturing of America, as presidents or chairmen of the boards of great corporations, have shoved the local segment of heavy industry out of the way to make room for their own executive suites. They have also taken over land previously dedicated to housing—of the rich and poor alike—for showplace headquarters in giant office buildings. Every year of the decade up to 1966, there was more *new* business office space constructed in New York City annually than in all of the principal cities of America put together. Any New Yorker wanting to play a guessing game can stand in front of a new edifice and ask himself, "What used to be here?"

Those who bemoan the loss of blue-collar jobs involved in manufacturing, forget that as the city has turned into the management center of the world, with the home offices of the nation's giant companies, it has attracted also the advertising agencies, promotional and statistical experts, architects and printers—all essential parts of the management complex. The financial stake in the new office building construction is so gigantic that the management industry, and all its satellites, are in New York to stay, whether or not they realize it. The new buildings are financed by mortgages and bond issues sponsored by the same financial institutions and banking interests that finance the manufacturing of America. There is an interlocking grip on the tenants, the management tycoons. One can recall when Park Avenue from 46 to 59 Streets was graced with the most luxurious hotels and apartment houses clustered anywhere. While still in the prime of life, they were demolished, one by one, to make room for the office buildings of the Lever House and Seagram Building type. The displaced rich residents of Park Avenue moved east and north into Yorkville, buying and demolishing or rebuilding the homes of the middle class or the poor. All a city government could do was to establish rent control and eviction rules that eased the burdens of those being relocated, without stopping the mass movement.

Again, along the East River from 42 to 57 Streets there had been cheap factory space, even slaughterhouses, the lowest use on the industrial totem pole. They were shoved out to make way for the headquarters of the United Nations, buildings for international trade and housing for those who go in

237

for cosmopolitan living. There, as elsewhere in Manhattan, the distinction between business and residential districts that had prevailed since the first zoning ordinance in 1916, began to disappear. Apartment houses and office buildings went up side by side even in Greenwich Village. Walking to work became so attractive that apartment rents could be raised to the point where they justified residence rather than industrial use. Carmine G. De Sapio's last political post, his district leadership in the Village, disappeared because his compatriots in the Little Italy section were displaced by upper-income housing. The same happened elsewhere, but with less to-do because the people involved were lesser known.

But displacement of the electorate by economic pressures was less a headache to the officeholder or political leader than the changes in the racial composition of the city. He always has been caught between the theoretical lack of race prejudice inherent in all the city and state laws and civic pronouncements, and the actual race prejudice which comes to the surface at any opportunity. New York had a tradition of liberalism and lack of prejudice of which its white residents were proud. No one thought they had reason to be otherwise, as long as the negroes remained cooped up in their Harlem ghetto, or a few other enclaves. When the dikes finally broke under irresistible pressure, and the low-income Negro population spilled out from Harlem into poor or middle class but previously white sections of the city, prejudice did rear its ugly head. The areas of conflict were broadened by the simultaneous increase in the immigration here from the island territory of Puerto Rico, of non-English speaking citizens of darker hue. Many white "liberals" withdrew their children from the public schools when the school population became mixed, either sending them to hastily-established private schools or else moving the whole family, lock, stock and barrel, to the still-white suburbs. As each white child withdrew, there was room for another Negro or Puerto Rican, increasing the percentage of non-whites and stimulating further white withdrawals, until the city school system wound up reflecting anything but the real racial balance of the community.

The school integration problem turned into as great a headache as the local politician is ever likely to encounter. The spotlight on school integration or segregation was nationwide, and those in New York, black or white, who derided the legalized situation in Alabama or Mississippi, were conscious that New York had de facto segregation, based on the housing pattern, which had been only partly eliminated in some areas, and even increased in others. It was the grade school that furnished the blankest of walls for it is the school designed to serve the immediate neighborhood, and in Harlem as elsewhere, the mother wants her six or seven-year-old home for lunch. Yet having him that close meant preservation of the de facto segregation that the awakening Negro leadership attacked both on the grounds of principle and of inferior educational exposure.

With much pain and turmoil, the city worked out a pattern for the transportation of children from one area where they lived, to another where they attended school, to the satisfaction of no one. Longer-range solutions remain in planning.

One answer on the part of the officeholders was to pour additional monies into the school system, to attract more qualified teachers into Harlem itself, to provide enriched programs, reading help, assistance for the non-English speaking child, all over the city, with a combination of everything in the schools marked by necessity for special service. It did not end segregation, but it did increase the educational chances of the child in school.

Much the same happened in the field of public housing, but with much less public exposure.

New York always has been ahead of all other cities in the scope of its public housing program. The early projects were all built by the city Housing Authority with federal or state credit, or by the Federal PWA, and were earmarked for the lowest income segment of the population, on the theory that they could least afford to pay the prices charged by the real estate interests. Unintentionally this weighted the potential as well as the actual tenant roster in favor of the Negro or the Puerto Rican, at the low end of the economy. This showed up particularly for projects built in existing slum neighborhoods, where the Negro and the Puerto Rican had moved into buildings vacated over the years by earlier immigrant groups. The Housing Authority, using city credit, later built a series of middle-income housing projects, in which the income limitations would not dictate the racial composition.

As the low-income housing was completed and tenanted, the racial imbalance became obvious and the city political leaders, from the Mayor down, were on the spot every time a proposed new low-income project came before the Board of Estimate for approval. Their white constituents bombarded them with demands for middle-income housing instead. The politicians found themselves in the position of favoring an expansion of the low-income program, with no sites for the new projects.

The leadership of the Negro community, instead of rallying to their aid, gave no help. It took a firm stand against building any more public housing in Harlem—no matter how run down a slum block was selected—on the grounds that the location dictated segregation. It also privately demanded that the politicians set up a sub-rosa-quota system for all the low-income housing to make sure that a cross section of tenants would be obtained. While a cross section of the population is certainly desirable, the New York State laws prohibit discrimination, and do not mandate integration. To set up a quota system was in flat violation of the anti-discrimination fiat. In practice it would have meant the earmarking of apartments by race, and holding them open, when vacated by a previous tenant, until an eligible family of the same race could be checked and housed. The leadership of the Negro community, as it existed then, pressed for this privately, but not publicly, for they did not dare tell their own people that they proposed cutting down the housing supply available to them.

It left the politicians holding the bag. For a short time they did impose an informal quota system, as requested, but dropped it as too hot to handle when they were challenged by the State Commission on Human Rights, the anti-discrimination enforcement agency.

The work by the city's officeholders in trying to adjust the city to its population changes has been constant, well-intentioned, and satisfactory to no one. The politician knows that no matter how sound or intelligent a program he evolves, it will be attacked on the one hand as too little, and on the other hand as too much. Yet he has kept working at it, because he has had no alternative. Such is the problem of the New York politician. Therein also lies the strength of the city's political system.